MATTHEW EADS

GRILL SEEKER

BASIC TRAINING FOR EVERYDAY GRILLING

FRONT TABLE BOOKS | AN IMPRINT OF CEDAR FORT, INC. | SPRINGVILLE, UTAH

ISBN 13: 978-1-4621-2342-1

Published by Front Table Books, an imprint of Cedar Fort, Inc.
2373 W. 700 S., Springville, UT 84663
Distributed by Cedar Fort, Inc., www.cedarfort.com

Library of Congress Cataloging-in-Publication Data

Names: Eads, Matthew, 1964-
Title: Grill seekers : basic training for everyday grilling / Matthew Eads.
Description: Springville, Utah : Front Table Books, An imprint of Cedar Fort, Inc., [2019]
Identifiers: LCCN 2018053307 (print) | LCCN 2019011433 (ebook) | ISBN 9781462130023 (epub, pdf, mobi) | ISBN 9781462123421 (perfect bound : alk. paper)
Subjects: LCSH: Barbecuing.
Classification: LCC TX840.B3 (ebook) | LCC TX840.B3 E22 2019 (print) | DDC 641.5/784--dc23
LC record available at https://lccn.loc.gov/2018053307

Cover design by Shawnda T. Craig
Page design by Shawnda T. Craig
Cover design © 2019 Cedar Fort, Inc.
Edited by Kaitlin Barwick

Printed in the United States of America

10 9 8 7 6 5 4 3 2

Printed on acid-free paper

CONTENTS

CHAPTER FOUR - BEEF 47

CHAPTER FIVE - POULTRY 69

CHAPTER SIX - PORK, VEAL, AND LAMB 89

INTRODUCTION

WHY DID I WRITE THIS BOOK?

Never in a million years did I think I would become an author. I was the high school student who routinely fell asleep in English class, being abruptly woken by the girl sitting behind me kicking my chair. Focusing on sports over academics, I wasn't all that interested in most things taught in class. Instead, I was always happier playing or watching a sport or grilling with my best friend, James. (If you're reading this buddy, stop laughing – I actually did write this!)

So why in the world did a classic academic underachiever like me decide to write a book? Over time, I've come to realize two things: First, grilling brings people together; people from all walks of life find common ground around a grill. Second, despite the unity to be found around a flame, too many resign their grill to burger or hot dog duty on a long weekend—not realizing the limitless possibilities a grill presents. I want to change that so others can get as much enjoyment from grilling as I do. The focus of this book is to show you that gourmet grilling doesn't have to be just a weekend activity. With my tips and tricks, you can craft amazing meals and amazing memories for family and friends every night of the week. The memories and the comradery that grilling has created for me, dating back to my teen years and throughout my time in the Marines, fuel my desire to spread my passion for outdoor cooking. They're also the reason I started the United by Flame movement on social media.

In this book, I'll cover some very easy recipes designed for everyday grilling; from appetizers to desserts, you'll get a bit of it all in this book. Yes, you *can* grill a banana split! In addition to the recipes, I'll also discuss different types of popular grills and some basic, yet essential, equipment for grillers of all skill levels. In the end, however, grilling is less about the type of grill or equipment you use and more about the results. And by "results" I don't just mean the food that comes off the grill. While that *is* a major component of grilling and the point of my simple recipes, what's also important is the experience of grilling. See, gourmet grilling isn't done out of necessity; it's a lifestyle, a process, and a skill that should be celebrated every day.

Happy grilling!

CHAPTER ONE

GETTING STARTED

DISCLOSURE
The Federal Trade Commission is very clear on disclosure laws regarding the transparency of paid advertisement. It's pretty clear cut, but not many abide by those rules—likely because they don't know the rules even exist. That said, I felt it imperative to mention that while I have been offered several cash endorsement deals to promote products in this book, I have declined all of them. To be clear, I haven't taken a single dime from any person or any brand in exchange for endorsement of any products in this book—I don't work that way. It's important for me to stay authentic so you can trust that the things I recommend in this book or on social media are products I actually use. My recommendations are not for sale, and they never will be.

ACKNOWLEDGMENT
I would like to extend a sincere thank you to a couple of great photographers that helped me with this book. Along with my own photographs, I was greatly assisted by Lauren Nagel from bonappeteach.com and Jessica Kim from jesskphotography.com with various shots throughout the book. Many thanks, ladies—your help is greatly appreciated.

TYPES OF GRILLS
We've come a long way since the caveman days of cooking over an open fire (though you *will* find a fun caveman technique on page 93. Outdoor cooking has evolved from a necessity to a hobby for many and even a competitive event for some. There are a number of different types of grills used today, all providing various advantages and, not surprisingly, all coming with some drawbacks. One of the biggest drawbacks is how confusing finding a grill that works for you can be. Don't worry, that's one of the reasons you bought this book—I've got you.

Below you'll find a brief description of some popular types of grills aimed at arming a new griller with the basic knowledge needed to make the best grill choice for his or her lifestyle and cooking needs. The most important part of choosing a grill is finding one you are comfortable operating on a regular basis. The "coolest" grill may be one that you'll dread using after the newness wears off because of the effort or time it takes to use and maintain it. And if you're not going to use it, you've just invested in a really cool lawn ornament and you still won't have dinner on the table. I use various grills for various things because it's my hobby and passion, but I recognize that won't be true for everyone (but if you get into the hobby with my help, feel free to blame me when explaining your second or third grill purchase to your significant other). Be practical with your decision, and don't be influenced by creative marketing or the coolest new gadget your neighbor has. In short, do you.

THE TRADITIONAL CHARCOAL GRILL
There's nothing more classic or timeless than the good old metal charcoal grill. These have been around for a long, long time and for good reason—they generally work well and are pretty budget

friendly. I say "generally" because there are some cheap knock-off brands on the market these days (below the $89 price point) that aren't built well and don't work well, and you'll be lucky if they last a single summer. In those cases, I'd say don't waste your time or money. These are commonly the models that are found at the local five-and-dime or on a display at the grocery store.

I recommend a more time-tested and consumer-proven model, like the classic Weber kettle or the traditional PK Grill, which can be purchased for between $200 and $350. For slightly more than what you'd pay for an el cheapo on the discount rack, you'll have a grill that will last you for thirty years or more. Indeed, there are plenty of 1950s vintage PKs and Webers in use today, passed down from one generation to the next like Grandma's old cast-iron skillet. These grills are lightweight, are heavily supported via online community groups, work extremely well for everyday grilling, and are portable enough for taking to the beach or a sporting event. They work well with either briquettes or lump charcoal, and the temperature control is managed by manipulating the intake and exhaust vents. Further, there is no shortage of accessories for either grill. While they *can* be used for smoking (large cuts like brisket and pork shoulders can indeed be smoked on a standard metal grill), they are generally better suited for straightforward grilling. Of course, there are exceptions to this, like with anything else. These grills offer quick heat-up and cool-down convenience for a budget that most are comfortable with. They do have some drawbacks. Most prominently, because of poor insulation they are affected by the weather, and a strong breeze or rain can significantly affect their performance.

THE CERAMIC GRILL

If you're shopping for a new grill this season, it would be hard not to come across the ceramic option during your research. Kamado-style cooking has gained massive popularity in recent years, and it has become all the rage due to the versatility these grills offer. There are three major players in the ceramic grill community: Big Green Egg, Primo, and Kamado Joe. All offer better all-weather performance than the standard metal grill, and each has an abundance of support via online forums and user groups.

Because two-zone cooking is essential to grilling, many prefer the Primo. Its patented oval design offers users better control and the widest variance for two—or even three—distinct temperature zones. It's also the only ceramic grill made in the United States. That said, if you're a gadget person, it's hard to beat the made-in-China Kamado Joe in terms of accessories and innovation. Indeed, Kamado Joe sets the pace for innovation. Being made in China isn't a bad thing, by the way—plenty of terrific products come from China—I only point it out as a comparison point. If you're looking for the largest online community, the Big Green Egg (made in Mexico) is the clear-cut favorite. Big Green Egg also benefits from the largest name recognition of the three and is likely the most readily available. You really can't go wrong with any of the three.

The main drawbacks to ceramic grills are cost and reaction time. They are slower to heat up and take longer to cool down. That said, users can grill, smoke, roast, and bake on these, and weather has little effect on their performance because they are so well insulated. Their superior insulation is also why they maintain moisture so well, so the days of dried-out meats from the grill are over. Like the standard metal grill, temperature adjustments are made via intake and exhaust vents. It's recommended that you use the slightly more expensive lump charcoal with these grills, and they *are* more expensive than the standard metal grill. Entry to market on a quality ceramic grill is about $800 at time of publication. I say "quality" because the market has recently flooded with knockoffs at big box stores that are much cheaper—for a reason. Be sure to check into the warranty and return policy on any of the discount ceramic grills, and even then, consider the logistics of returning such a heavy grill.

THE GAS GRILL

As much as I, and others like me, enjoy stoking up the coals or wood splits and cooking over live fire, there's no denying that gas grills are still king. Sales numbers year after year support this, and there are plenty of reasons to cook on a quality gas grill. Most notably is the convenience. With the turn of a knob, your grill is ready to go. Unlike charcoal grills that use airflow through intake and exhaust vents to control temperature, gas grills achieve this by introducing more or less gas into a burner when the knob is turned. When you're done cooking on a gas grill, you simply turn it off. No excessive ash cleanup, no extended cool-down period— it's literally like using the gas range top in your kitchen . . . kinda.

Gas grills do come with some drawbacks, though. Charcoal purists would say the flavor from a gas grill is never as good as that from a charcoal grill. I don't buy into this completely, especially for things like burgers, hot dogs, and thinner cuts of meat. The kinds of foods that people cook most often aren't over charcoal long enough to take on much, if any, flavor from the coals, so in large part that's just purist talk. I like to think of myself as a realist as opposed to a purist, and realistically, a gas grill will do 95 percent of what a charcoal grill will do, while providing more convenience and requiring less cleanup. I'm convinced that I could make almost anything on my gas grill and 99 out of 100 people wouldn't be able to tell that it wasn't done on a charcoal grill.

There *are* some important things to consider when buying a gas grill in order to prevent wasting your money on disappointment. Unlike charcoal models, where a cheap unit will get the job done temporarily but won't last long, a cheap gas grill won't get the job done OR last long. I've tested countless budget gas grills, and most of them simply don't get hot enough to create the kind of sear that you get from charcoal. Add to that the flare-ups that happen with most budget model gas grills, and the entire experience is underwhelming and disappointing. A high-end gas grill can set you back a decent amount of scratch, but it'll last a lifetime and produce the type of heat needed for excellent food. The list of manufacturers for high-quality gas grills is short, and I've had the best performance from the Lynx grills lineup. The trident burner they offer is capable of producing heat of over 1200°F, which is more than any backyard or professional chef would need—unless they're planning to forge some metal while their burgers are cooking. Additionally, this intense heat all but eliminates flare-ups. That said, it's also capable of very low temperatures for grilling delicate things like fish. It's made in America and is backed by a warranty that's second to none. Add to that the versatile Lynx lineup, and you can outfit an outdoor kitchen that would fit just fine into an *Architectural Digest* spread.

THE BARREL COOKER

Barrel cooking has been around for many, many years, but it has only recently become popular in the mainstream. Initially, these smokers were built by do-it-yourselfers making use of old 55-gallon drums and were dubbed Ugly Drum Smokers or UDSs. While many still make use of 55-gallon drums today, the UDS has been refined over the years, and now there are a number of manufacturers that build out-of-the-box-ready drum smokers at price points ranging from sub $200 on the low end to about $800 for a premium model.

Barrel cookers are used primarily for smoking, but some can also be used for grilling in the right configuration. What makes these cookers unique is the way meat is placed in the barrels. Aside from the traditional placement on a wire rack, barrel cookers also allow users to hang food from hooks inside the barrel for a nice smoke bath. The hanging method accomplishes two goals: First, by hanging vertically as opposed to sitting horizontally, the capacity of the cooker is greatly increased. It wouldn't be difficult to hang sixteen racks of pork spare ribs in a full-sized barrel cooker. Second, and equally (if not more) important, is the effect the juices dripping on the coals has. The food hangs high enough above the coals so as not to burn, but when the juices drip onto the coals, they create steam, which helps cook and infuse flavor into the meat. Beyond that, it's just a fun way to cook! I use this style of cooker all the time at tailgate events, and the crowd is always mesmerized by this method.

I've used all kinds of barrel smokers, and the budget-friendly brands work well, some being built better than others, which leads to a longer service life. For someone who is serious about the craft of barrel smoking, I'd suggest investing in a higher-end model. Both Gateway Drum Smokers and Hunsaker Smokers make top-shelf barrel cookers that will last a long, long time and have plenty of capacity. Hunsaker may get a slight advantage for its vortex fire box, but Gateway offers the option of having it custom painted, which can also be fun. Really, you can't go wrong with either unit, both made in America.

The downside of the barrel cooker is that while it can be used for grilling, that's not its main purpose, so doing a burger or steak isn't as easy as it is with other types of grills. If your main interest is smoking meat, while only occasionally grilling, this might be a great option. On the other hand, if your main interest is grilling, this probably isn't the right type of cooker for you.

THE PELLET GRILL

With the help of clever marketing, widespread availability, and ease of use, pellet grilling has gained popularity at the pace of a stock car circling a NASCAR super speedway. Though it is similar to a gas grill, "purists" discount this style grill because it doesn't use charcoal or wood—or even gas. Instead, it uses compressed wood pellets to generate heat and smoke. This type of grill has truly broadened the field of users who enjoy and excel at outdoor cooking.

The grill requires electricity to run an auger that feeds wood pellets to an igniter. Unlike other grills that use a vent system or gas valve to control temperature, the pellet grill generally has a touch pad or dial to select the desired temperature, and the grill then essentially operates like an indoor oven, only outdoors. Set and forget is the concept, and people have definitely embraced it. Pricing on these units ranges dramatically, and there is no shortage of suppliers for these grills. Going cheap on one of these may not be advisable, given the number of moving parts and opportunities for failure, so consider spending a little extra for a higher-end model. Companies like Yoder Smokers and Green Mountain Grills make extremely well-built products. Similar to the barrel cooker, the downside to these units is their poor grilling performance. Most manufacturers will claim that their pellet grill can both smoke and sear, and that may be technically true—depending on your idea of what searing is. The bottom line is that these units make much better smokers than grills.

BASIC EQUIPMENT

So you've bought a grill—now what? It may be tempting to just fire it up and start cooking, but before you do, let's get familiar with some essential tools of the trade. These pieces of equipment will help ensure you're getting the best results every time. Below is my list of basic equipment every novice griller should invest in before turning on his or her grill. (We'll cover turning on your grill in the next section.)

ELECTRONIC LEAVE-IN THERMOMETERS

These types of units are designed to insert a probe into the meat and *leave it in* so you can monitor the internal temperature of the meat throughout the cooking cycle. They allow for the cook to closely track temperature over time to ensure a perfect doneness without over or under cooking. If you've ever dubiously poked a cut of meat on your grill wondering, *Is it done yet?*, these probes are for you. Plenty of people will tell you they don't need a thermometer because they know how to cook or they go by feel. To that I say, *good luck.* I'm not too proud to use technology in order to ensure a well-cooked piece of meat. I'll take a delicious meal over my pride any day.

Generally, these models come with two channels—and sometimes four or even six. By "channel" I mean the ability to read different temperatures at the same time, without moving a single channel probe. Having two channels allows one probe to be inserted into the meat, while the other is placed in the grill to allow for monitoring of the cooking chamber temperature. Extra channels of course mean the ability to monitor more than one piece of meat at a time, while still monitoring the temperature of the cooking chamber.

Why would you need to monitor grill temperature, since most grills come with a built-in thermometer? Good question. Here's one of the secrets of great grilling—never trust the thermometer than comes with your grill. Those analog gauges (no matter the grill's price point) are often purchased by the grill's manufacturer from a lowest-price-point third party and are notoriously inaccurate. Also, they read temperature in the dome or lid of the grill, where they are usually mounted, not at the grill's cooking surface, where your food is located. Trust me on this one: pay no attention to those built-in grill gauges. Instead, get yourself a dependable electronic thermometer, and place one probe inside the grill near where your food will cook and another into the food to read internal food temperature.

In most cases, a two-channel will work just fine, but I recommend at least a four-channel model, and I strongly prefer a six channel. Why would you need more than two temperature readings? A couple of reasons actually. First, and most obvious, you'll often want to monitor more than one protein at a time (multiple steaks being reverse seared at once, for example). In that instance, having extra temperature probes is nice because each steak will cook at a slightly different rate. Second, extra channels are useful for cooking large cuts of meat. A brisket, for example, can weigh over 15 pounds and have varying degrees of thickness, so you may want to monitor the temperature in more than one spot. Finally, and one of my favorite uses for my six-channel FireBoard electric temperature indicator, is the ability to check my grills for hot spots. All grills have hot spots, or areas on the cooking surface that get hotter than other areas. By placing the temperature probes around a grill's cooking surface, you'll better understand how your grill behaves. Understanding your grills heat dispersion will allow you to avoid burning your food and embarrassing yourself in front of your friends. Not that I have ever ruined a several-hundred-dollar prime rib in front of a house full of people or anything.

Nowadays, most all of these types of thermometers have some sort of app associated with them that allows for monitoring via a smart phone. Expectedly, some apps work better than others, so keep that in mind and do some research when you're selecting what's right for you. Pricing on a quality thermometer ranges from about $70 to $150. There are a few that I recommend. For a simple two-channel, the Thermoworks Smoke is a nice option and works well, but it's a bit overpriced in my opinion. If you want to expand your capabilities to a four-channel, I recommend the Maverick XR-50 (which is also the lowest price point of the thermometers I recommend). And, of course, the king of leave-in thermometers, which provides the most flexibility, is the budget-friendly six-channel FireBoard Labs smart thermometer.

QUICK-READ THERMOMETER

In contrast to the probe-style of thermometer, the quick-read version is not left in during the cooking process. Instead, this style of probe is inserted briefly into the food, and within a couple of seconds you'll have an accurate reading of your food's internal temperature. This tool is what I would consider a must-have for all cooks at every level. It's very versatile and very dependable. My only regret is that my dad didn't have one of these when he grilled hockey pucks throughout my childhood—he told us they were hamburgers, but I promise they met all NHL regulations. Dad did most everything exceptionally well, but grilling wasn't one of them. In any case, do yourself a favor and buy one of these gadgets ASAP. Your family and anyone you cook for will thank you.

A quality instant-read thermometer runs about $100 and will read temperature in less than three seconds. Why not just use the leave-in style? Fair question—the answer is that the wires and the thickness of the probes often don't lend themselves to thinner steaks or burgers that might be flipped often. In those cases, the quick read is the better option. I've used a number of them over the years and have had the best luck with the Thermoworks Mk4, a terrific value.

TONGS

Tongs are absolutely essential for grilling, as you can imagine. The problem is that there are so many on the market that choosing which one to buy can be a bit daunting. Sadly, most of the sets you find are flawed in some way. The most common problems are sturdiness and ergonomics. When looking for tongs, find yourself a pair that is long enough that you don't burn your hand when turning meat, has a strong enough spring to operate the action effectively, and fits your hand. I wouldn't recommend the cheapo tongs you find online. Spend a couple extra bucks for a quality set that will last for years. When I say "extra" I'm not talking about much; for about $15 you can get a great set of tongs that work well and will last a long time. I've had great luck with the OXO brand, but there are plenty others that do the job as well. What's most important to remember is to use tongs when turning your meat, and *never* use those ridiculous pronged BBQ forks. As you penetrate your meat with these forks, you are releasing the juices from the meat, and that's a no-no.

SMOKE TUBE

For those gas grillers out there, these tubes can be your best friend. One of the biggest knocks on gas grills is that they don't produce the flavor that you get from a wood-fired or charcoal grill. That opinion is debatable to be sure, but a smoke tube can certainly help to bridge that gap. These devices house wood chips or compressed wood pellets and slowly burn them, producing a nice clean smoke to fill your grill and provide that smoky flavor for just about anything you have on your gas grill. Steaks, fish, and so on will all benefit from a smoke tube, assuming a smoky profile is something you desire. These tubes usually run around $15 and come in various sizes from various manufacturers. Of course, some work better than others, but for the most part they're all very similar in design. I've used the A-MAZE-N tubes with great success, but there are plenty of others that work just as well.

WOOD CHUNKS

For many of my recipes, you'll see me reference the addition of wood chunks to the coals. You'll notice I recommend placing the wood chunks on top of the hot coals in my recipes, which is great for a hint of smoke flavor. For a more robust smoke flavor, closer to a traditional BBQ profile, try placing the wood chunks deep in a bed of unlit charcoal and topping with some hot charcoal. The purpose is obviously to introduce a nice smoke flavor to the food you're cooking, but don't mistake chunks for chips. Both are pretty readily available, but the chips burn up very quickly and don't perform as well as the chunks.

You'll also read in various places that you should soak wood chunks in water before using them; the idea is that a wet chunk will smolder longer. While the concept makes sense, in practice it's sort of a myth. Soaking a wood chunk for even several hours doesn't really do much because the water simply doesn't penetrate deep enough. So save the time and hassle, and don't bother with that practice. It's also important to remember not to get too carried away with the amount of wood chunks you use. In most cases, one or two chunks is plenty. If it starts to look like you upended a wood chipper into your grill, it's time to stop. For an entertaining story about how I learned that lesson, read the blog post on my website, grillseeker.com, called "How Not to Smoke a Brisket."

GRILL BASKET

While maybe not a must-have, a grill basket is certainly nice to have. I grill a lot of vegetables, and without a basket, they tend to fall through the grill grates and burn to a crisp, creating a mess you'll have to clean up later. The baskets come in various shapes, some have handles and others don't, and they are similar to a colander with slightly bigger holes. This allows your veggies (or spaghetti, see my recipe for that on page 97 to cook over the grill without the food falling through the grate. Pricing on these ranges from $17 to $70, which is a big swing. I wouldn't spend $70 on one of these personally and don't recommend you do either. This is one of those items that I recommend buying a low-cost model and simply replacing it when needed. Properly maintained, even the cheap versions should last several years. Do yourself a favor and give your basket a quick spray of cooking spray before cooking anything in it, as food tends to stick to these.

TECHNIQUES

You've got your grill, you've got your basic equipment, and you've got your meat—it's finally time to start cooking.

Almost.

Before you fire anything up, let's go over the basic techniques that will help you keep your dinners delicious and avoid the unfortunate shoe-leather phase so many grillers go through. Don't worry— I'll talk you through it.

LIGHTING YOUR CHARCOAL GRILL

Let's get started with the basics: lighting your grill. Lighting a gas model is simple and usually done by the turn of the knob. This convenience is one of the most attractive parts of a gas grill. Lighting a charcoal grill can be a bit more challenging for a first timer, and some have even said they intimidated by it. No need for intimidation! This is a simple process that even the most inexperienced griller can master in no time. First things first: never use lighter fluid. Lighter fluid leaves a chemical taste on your food, even after it's burned off the charcoal, and if you use a ceramic grill, that fluid will penetrate the porous ceramic and your food will forever taste like gasoline.

Having established the no-lighter-fluid standard, I recommend three different techniques for lighting charcoal. The first is done using a charcoal chimney, which can be purchased for around $20. This tool allows you to dump charcoal into the chimney's top half while using old newspaper or junk mail in the bottom of the chimney as an ignition source. Light the paper, and within minutes, the coals are ready to go. Simply dump them into the grill, and you're all set. There are some drawbacks to this method, including the sparks that often jump out as the lit coals are being dumped into the grill. There is also the issue of where to set the extremely hot chimney down after you dump the coals into the grill. I don't recommend these for those who have a composite deck, as the sparks that jump from the chimney can often melt the composite surface.

The next option is an electric lighter, like the Looftlighter. Looftlighter was the original electric lighter, but it's been knocked off many times by other manufacturers. This device uses extremely hot air to light your lump or briquettes. Using the Looftlighter or a similar lighter will allow you to pour the unlit charcoal into the grill (preventing the sparks that happen with the chimney method) and light the coals within minutes. Like the chimney, this method has some drawbacks. As mentioned, this is an electric lighter, so if you don't have an outlet near your grill, the lighter is unusable. There's always the extension cord option, but I'm a realist and understand that most people are not going to want to go to that effort.

The final option I recommend is a small fire starter that can be purchased online and in some retail stores. Using this method allows the unlit charcoal to be poured into the grill, again avoiding the sparks from the chimney because the charcoal is not yet lit. There are several different types of fire starters—though many are chemical based, and I don't recommend those for the same reason I don't recommend lighter fluid. Instead, I prefer to use the natural starters that are made of wood shavings and resemble small bird nests. These things work extremely well but can get expensive over time. They can be purchased for about 40 cents each—which isn't terrible, but the cost can add up if you grill frequently.

TWO-ZONE COOKING

Now that we know how to light the coals, let's talk about how to set up the grill. One of the most common mistakes among novice outdoor cooks is setting up the grill with an even distribution of coals over the entire grill and cooking their food solely over direct heat. It's comparable to cooking a meal on a stovetop burner using only the highest setting. On a grill, cooking exclusively over super-hot direct heat leads to flare-ups and food that is often overcooked on the outside and undercooked on the inside or—even worse—overcooked on the outside AND inside. Remember those hockey puck burgers I mentioned my dad turning out? That's a result of trying to cook a burger all the way through using direct heat.

For roughly 90 percent of what the typical backyard cook is going to make on the grill, there should be two separate areas of heat established in the grill. This is commonly referred to as *two-zone heating*, and it's one of the fundamentals of grilling. Just as the name implies, there are two zones: a very hot direct zone just above the heat source (coals on a charcoal grill or flames on a gas grill) and a cooler indirect zone away from the heat source. In the direct zone, conduction heat transfer is used for fast cooking and searing. In the indirect zone, convection heating is used and acts more like an oven to slowly raise the temperature of the food.

With a two-zone setup, burgers that could be used in a Stanley Cup game are a thing of the past. In most of the grilling recipes in this book, your cooking should happen over indirect heat. This allows slow cooking of your meat—for your entire burger, steak, chop, and so on to gradually and evenly come up to the desired temperature. Additionally, you'll avoid those flare-ups and overcooking the outside of the meat. For the most part, but not always, direct heat will only be used at the very end of your cook in order to get that nice char that looks beautiful and adds an intense amount of flavor to whatever you're serving.

To set up your charcoal grill for two-zone cooking, pile all of your coals on one side of the grill; this will be the direct heat, or hot zone. The other side will have no coals and will be your indirect heat, or cool zone. For a gas grill, only light half of the burners and leave the other half turned off to form hot and cool zones.

Now that you have your grill set up for two-zone heat, the last step before you start cooking is to find out the temperature of your cool zone using one of the recommended thermometers we discussed earlier.

DIRECT HEAT
Just as the name applies, direct heat is that heat directly above the hot coals on a charcoal grill, or the lit burners on a gas model. This is the area of the grill that's the hottest. It's used for searing the outside of meats and vegetables through conduction heating and for cooking hot and fast in the case of thin cuts of meat. Be careful of flare-ups that are prone to happen when cooking directly over the heat source. As the fats or oils render and drip onto the flame, they can flare up like lighter fluid. (Important note: As stated earlier, I don't advocate using lighter fluid, *ever*.)

INDIRECT HEAT
Just the opposite of direct heat, indirect heat is convection heating, which is used for most larger cuts of meat by placing the food away from the direct heat zone to allow for a gradual increase in internal temperature. Many of the recipes in this book call for starting with indirect heat and finishing with direct heat. Find more on that method in the reverse sear section below. The bottom line: indirect heat is like making your grill into an outdoor oven, while direct heat is like making your grill into an outdoor stove burner.

REVERSE SEAR
You'll see me reference this technique often throughout this book because it's really the basic foundation of cooking any thick cut of meat. With this method, you'll be able to achieve the flavors and appearances of food purchased at high-end restaurants.

Most people start with the searing process; I couldn't disagree more with that technique for most meats. Searing first "to lock in the juices" can leave you with gray overcooked edges on your steak and an undercooked, raw middle. Try cooking a boneless skinless chicken breast using only direct heat; it will be, in a word, terrible. In order to get the center of the meat to a safe eating temperature, you have to dry out the outside of the meat, creating a piece of drywall where poultry once was. By using the reverse sear technique, you'll end up with even doneness throughout your steak, chicken, or pork. If you master this, every bite of your protein will be perfection—a slight crunch from the crust on the outside while the center of the meat still melts in your mouth.

Reverse searing is achieved by placing your food over indirect heat to start and then moving it to direct heat to finish the cooking process—reversing the typical searing method. Doing so allows the inside of the meat to gradually rise to desired temperature so that the doneness is uniform from edge to edge. Then, at the end of the process, the meat is introduced to extremely high temperatures of direct heat to produce a char on the outside that packs a ton of flavor due to the Maillard reaction. For a greater explanation of the Maillard reaction, see my blog post about it on grillseeker.com.

· CHAPTER TWO ·

THE BASICS

APPLE CINNAMON BRINE

If your childhood was anything like mine, you grew up eating pork chops that could double as replacement soles for your worn-out sneakers. To be fair, back then the USDA recommended cooking cuts of pork to 160°F. To each their own, but for most of us a pork chop cooked to a 160-degree internal temperature is, in a word, inedible. Luckily, though the safe temperature for ground pork still remains at 160°F, the safe temperature for pork chops has since been adjusted to 145°F, and at that temperature a high-end cut of pork is very juicy.

For those who don't have the budget for $50.00-per-pound Kurobuta pork chops, this brine will make any grocery-store $2.00-per-pound chop taste like a million bucks.

6 cups water

3 cups apple cider or apple juice

2 cups sugar

6 cinnamon sticks

2 Tbsp. black peppercorns

1 Tbsp. whole cloves

1 Tbsp. salt

2 bay leaves

zest of 1 orange

1. Combine water and apple cider in large stockpot and bring to rolling boil.
2. Add remaining ingredients. Reduce heat to medium, cover, and let boil for 10 minutes.
3. Remove from heat and allow to cool (covered) to room temperature.
4. Strain the brine into a suitable container.

TIP:
THIS IS EXCELLENT FOR PORK CHOPS, BUT DON'T STOP THERE. TRY IT WITH PORK RIBS, WHOLE CHICKENS, AND CORNISH HENS.

BBQ RUB

Every grill seeker needs a go-to BBQ rub. It must enhance the natural flavors of the meat— without overpowering the senses—and offer just enough heat to keep it interesting. Some people spend years developing the perfect combination of ingredients. Rubs are a closely guarded secret among the BBQ community; some are passed down through generations. Trust me, at griller gatherings more fights break out over paprika to garlic powder ratios than politics.

What are you to do if your ancestors weren't grillers? Well, you look like honest people, so I'll trust you with my personal recipe. This is a great basic rub that complements most meats and adds just enough kick to keep each bite interesting. The best part about this recipe? It's a base. Feel free to add new ingredients or alter the proportions to craft the perfect rub for you and your family.

½ cup light brown sugar

½ cup smoked paprika

1 Tbsp. freshly ground black pepper

1 Tbsp. kosher salt

1 Tbsp. ground savory

1 Tbsp. chili powder

1 Tbsp. garlic powder

1 Tbsp. onion powder

1 tsp. ground cayenne pepper

1 tsp. dried thyme

1. Using a medium-sized mixing bowl, combine all ingredients and whisk together until thoroughly blended.

2. Transfer into a glass or plastic airtight container, and store in a cool, dry place. Rub will last about 3 months before flavors start to subside.

BLUE CHEESE PEPPERCORN BUTTER

There's only one thing better than a perfectly cooked cut of meat: a perfectly cooked cut of meat with a big pat of butter melting on top of it. Butter is the base of many dishes, but we often overlook its importance to the meals we prepare. It's a great complement to meat on its own, but infused with a little something extra—like herbs or spices—it can totally transform the dishes you cook.

Don't spend your hard-earned money on the expensive infused butters you find at gourmet stores when it's so easy and quick to make your own at home. I'll walk you through the basics of creating a great infused butter here, and once you've mastered this recipe, you can experiment with different flavor combinations. Infused butter is a breeze to make and is sure to impress your guests. It even makes a thoughtful and useful gift that will thrill the gourmands in your life.

1 cup unsalted butter, room temperature

1¾ cups (8 oz.) blue cheese

1 Tbsp. olive oil

1 Tbsp. fresh black peppercorns, cracked

1 tsp. sea salt

2 cloves garlic, minced

2 Tbsp. finely chopped fresh parsley

1. Remove butter from refrigerator and allow it to naturally come to room temperature (usually takes a few hours). Don't try using the microwave—the microwave will melt it, not soften it.

2. Place the softened butter in a mixing bowl. Using a fork, smash in remaining ingredients, allowing some of the blue cheese to remain in small chunks.

3. Using a rubber spatula, scrape the butter mixture onto parchment paper. Roll the parchment around the butter, forming it into a log with a 1½-inch diameter. Twist the ends to seal.

4. Refrigerate butter until it is firm and can be sliced.

COMPOUND HERB BUTTER

Let's get the obvious question out of the way: Why do we make fancy butter when we can buy regular butter anywhere? Because adding fresh herbs and lemon elevates this kitchen staple into an essential, put-it-on-everything treat. You can buy pricey compound butters like this from a gourmet store, but why? My recipe is easy to make, is absolutely delicious, and will save you a ton of money.

This butter is the perfect addition to a steak, seafood, some Texas toast, or grilled veggies. Even the veggie hater in your house will be a convert when you top greens with some of this compound butter. The possibilities are endless, and that's one of the reasons I like it so much. Well, that, and it's insanely good. For a special treat, use some high-quality butter, like Kerry Gold or Finlandia craft small-batch butter for this recipe.

1 cup unsalted butter, room temperature

1 Tbsp. olive oil

1 Tbsp. rosemary salt (page 19)

2 cloves garlic, minced

zest from 1 lemon

2 Tbsp. finely chopped fresh parsley

2 Tbsp. finely chopped fresh chives

2 Tbsp. finely chopped fresh rosemary

1. Remove butter from refrigerator and allow it to naturally come to room temperature (usually takes a few hours). Don't try using the microwave—the microwave will melt it, not soften it.

2. Place the softened butter in a mixing bowl and stir in remainig ingredients. Mix well.

3. Using a rubber spatula, scrape the butter mixture onto parchment paper. Roll the parchment around the butter, forming it into a log with a 1½-inch diameter. Twist the ends to seal.

4. Refrigerate butter until it is firm and can be sliced.

TIP:
IF YOU LIKE SOME HEAT,
TRY ADDING A TEASPOON
OF CAYENNE PEPPER.

NJP RUB

Marines love a good competition. Back when I was in the Corps, plenty of downtime was spent watching my fellow marines compete to prove their manhood, doing pull-ups, push-ups, or whatever feats they could think of. After the physical part of the competition, there was usually a "food" round. The guys would gulp down hot sauce or eat hot peppers to determine who had the toughest taste buds.

Personally, I'm not a fan of eating anything that's going to make my mouth numb for a week. I love some heat, but only if the flavor is good. Heat for heat's sake doesn't improve a meal. That's why I've created this NJP (non-judicial punishment) rub—it's hot enough to impress my brothers in the Corps, but it doesn't skimp on flavor.

If you feel the need for some heat in your next meal, try this rub on skirt steak, poultry, or seafood. It's good training for your taste buds (but it won't help you with your pull-ups).

½ cup finely ground kosher salt

½ cup finely ground black pepper

3 Tbsp. Hungarian hot paprika

3 Tbsp. garlic powder

2 Tbsp. jalapeño powder

1 Tbsp. red pepper flakes

1. Using a medium-sized mixing bowl, combine all ingredients and whisk together until thoroughly blended.
2. Transfer into a glass or plastic airtight container, and store in a cool, dry place. Rub will last about 3 months before flavors start to subside.

TIP:
TRY THIS ON YOUR BREAKFAST, ESPECIALLY ON THOSE OVER-EASY EGGS OR PORK SAUSAGE PATTIES.

PORK AND POULTRY RUB

Chicken and pork sometimes get a bad rap for being bland. I'm here to tell you that your protein is only as bland as you make it. There are lots of cooking techniques (some of which you'll find on other pages) that can transform a dish from bland to beautiful. But sometimes you don't have time for a drawn-out fancy cooking technique. Sometimes you're tired after a long day and just want to get dinner on the table—*now*.

This pork and poultry rub is the perfect "easy way" solution to make your food flavorful. I've used paprika, sage, and cayenne to bring out subtle smoky flavors in the meat, plus a little garlic powder because you can never have enough garlic. It will keep for weeks in an airtight container. Just pull it out, sprinkle it on your protein of choice, and enjoy a quick meal that tastes like you've been working on it all day.

¼ cup brown sugar

¼ cup smoked paprika

3 Tbsp. coarse sea salt

2 Tbsp. freshly ground black pepper

2 Tbsp. garlic powder (not salt)

2 Tbsp. onion powder

2 tsp. cumin

2 tsp. cayenne pepper

2 tsp. dried sage

1. Using a medium-sized mixing bowl, combine all ingredients and whisk together until thoroughly blended.

2. Transfer into a glass or plastic airtight container, and store in a cool, dry place. Rub will last about 3 months before flavors start to subside.

ROASTED GARLIC AND DILL BUTTER

One of my favorite herbs is also one of the trickiest to work with. Dill, while a great complement to seafood and vegetables, is easy to overuse. But that didn't stop me from finding a way to incorporate it into a delectable butter. After a bit of trial and error, I determined the perfect amount of dill to add to this butter. It brightens up the flavors of delicate proteins and vegetables without overpowering them.

Be sure to use unsalted butter when you're preparing this—salted butter with rosemary salt will have you rushing for a glass of water. It also pays to invest in some gourmet small-batch butter from a farmer's market, which will give this compound butter a luxurious texture. Garlic and shallots pair well with the dill and make this a perfect complement to wild-caught fish or spring vegetables.

3 cloves garlic

drizzle of olive oil

pinch of salt

½ cup unsalted butter, room temperature

½ shallot, finely minced

¼ cup finely chopped dill and 2 whole pieces of dill

1 Tbsp. rosemary salt (page 19)

½ tsp. garlic powder

zest and juice of 1 lemon

1. Set oven to 350°F.
2. Place garlic cloves on a foil-lined tray and drizzle with olive oil and a pinch of salt. Place in oven and roast for 15 minutes or until browned and soft. Remove from oven and allow to cool.
3. Roughly smash cooled garlic cloves with a fork.
4. In a medium-sized mixing bowl, add smashed garlic, butter, minced shallot, chopped dill (not the whole pieces), rosemary salt, garlic powder, lemon zest, and lemon juice. Using a fork, thoroughly mix ingredients to a consistent blend.
5. Using a rubber spatula, scrape the butter mixture onto parchment paper and form into a log shape. Top with whole pieces of dill.
6. Roll the parchment around the butter, forming it into a log with a 1½-inch diameter. Twist the ends to seal. Store in refrigerator until firm.
7. Serve with your favorite dish. This goes great with seafood, especially salmon or scallops, or any roasted spring vegetables.

ROSEMARY SALT

I was spending a ton of money on this store-bought salt because I use it on just about everything. I love it on roasted potatoes, but it's good on steak, pork, even mac and cheese. Pricing on this is similar to the smoked salts you can buy commercially, hitting the pocketbook at about $35 per pound. It's always cleverly packaged so it doesn't seem that expensive, and if used only on occasion, it's fine. But I love it and want to use it more than what's economically reasonable.

After spending way more on this stuff than I care to admit, I decided to make it myself. It took a bit of experimenting to sort it out, but what you'll find below is perfect (one of the few "hacks" that are actually better than the original). A couple key points to remember: First, doing this on a charcoal grill gives an added layer of flavor. Second, it's important to finely grind a portion of the rosemary as described below to give the salt that perfect mix of coarse and fine. Stored in an airtight jar, it can keep for weeks.

½ cup sea salt flakes

¾ cup rosemary, removed from stalks

zest from 1 lemon

---

1. Preheat grill to 200°F.
2. Line a tray with foil. The foil will make it easy to pour the mix into the grinder later.
3. Mix salt, ½ cup rosemary, and lemon zest on one side of the foil-lined tray. Place the other ¼ cup rosemary on other side of tray. Be very careful to not mix them together at this point.

4. Place in grill using indirect heat for 20 minutes.
5. Remove from grill and let cool to room temperature.
6. Add the salt, ½ cup rosemary, and lemon zest mix (not the ¼ cup rosemary) to a coffee grinder and blend coarsely. Be careful not to overgrind, or you'll end up with powder. Pour into a container.
7. Blend remaining ¼ cup rosemary in coffee grinder until it becomes a powder.
8. Pour into same container with the coarse mixture, cover, and shake to blend.
9. Store in an airtight container.

TIP: WHEN POURING INTO THE COFFEE GRINDER, FORM THE FOIL INTO A FUNNEL FOR AN EASY AND MESS-FREE POUR.

SEEKER SAUCE

Seemingly every fast-food burger joint has some sort of secret sauce, no one more discernable than another. Mostly they all taste like Thousand Island dressing to me, and while I like Thousand Island dressing, I wanted to create something with a bit more pizzazz. After a handful of tries to get the proportions right, I fell in love with the below and use it on fries, burgers, scrambled eggs, and any number of sandwiches. As condiments go, this will soon be your go-to for its versatility. Dare I say, it may even rival ranch dressing?

1 cup mayonnaise

2 Tbsp. ketchup

2 Tbsp. Dijon mustard

2 small kosher dill pickles

1 Tbsp. pickle juice

2 tsp. Worcestershire sauce

1 tsp. salt

½ tsp. sweet paprika

1. Combine all ingredients in a food processor and pulse several times until mixture is smooth and pickles are completely incorporated.

2. Transfer into a sealable glass jar or squeezable squirt bottle. Store in refrigerator until expiration date of mayonnaise.

SMOKED CHIPOTLE AIOLI

Chipotle peppers pack a ton of flavor into a tiny package. They bring heat and depth of flavor to any dish. Don't worry, though, this aioli isn't too hot to handle, because the sour cream and mayonnaise balance out the harsher edges of the chipotle.

The key to this aioli is hickory salt, which is just as easy to make as this aioli! You'll want to get ready to put this on just about everything. Chipotle aioli is a great addition to meats (especially less-flavorful cuts like London broil), vegetables, and sandwiches. Or you could just do what we do at our house: pour the aioli into a bowl and eat it on tortilla chips.

1½ cups mayonnaise

½ cup sour cream

2 chipotle peppers in adobo sauce

1 Tbsp. adobo sauce

1 Tbsp. hickory smoked salt (page 22)

1. Put all ingredients into a bullet-style blender or food processor and pulse till evenly incorporated.
2. Serve room temperature or slightly warm.
3. Store in refrigerator in an airtight container until expiration date of sour cream or mayonnaise, whichever comes first.

TIP:
DON'T THROW OUT THE PEPPERS YOU DON'T USE; THEY FREEZE WELL, AND YOU CAN THAW THEM OUT WHEN YOU WANT TO MAKE THIS DELICIOUS SAUCE AGAIN.

SMOKED SALT

I'm the kind of guy who likes salt on everything—like, I salt my salt. I'm also the kind of guy who loves to smoke just about everything, from butter, cheese, and nuts to a big fat brisket and all things in between. That said, what better way to combine the two loves than to create some really unique flavors by smoking salt?

Sure, you can buy commercial smoked salt off the shelf, but you might need to take out a second mortgage if you plan to use it on more than just a special occasion. Jokes aside, smoked salts sell for around $3.50 an ounce. Clever packaging makes this stuff seem affordable, and while I'm no math major, I believe this comes out to be about $56.00 a pound . . . for salt! No thanks.

You can make this yourself, have a ton of fun doing it, and customize your flavor profiles for about eight bucks a pound based on the wood or pellets you use. For salt, I like to use apple, hickory, or mesquite wood chunks or pellets.

1 lb. coarse sea salt

your choice of flavored wood chunks or pellets

CHARCOAL-FUELED GRILL

1. Set your grill up for two-zone heat at 250°F.

2. Spread salt evenly on a foil-lined baking tray.

3. Drop 1 or 2 wood chunks (not chips—they burn out way too quickly) onto your hot coals.

4. Place salt into the indirect side of grill, close lid, and let smoke for about 30 minutes. The salt will change color slightly during this process.

5. Remove salt from grill, and let cool to room temperature.

6. Form foil lining into a funnel and pour into a glass jar with a good sealable lid.

7. Store in a cool, dry place for as long as you like. If it gets clumpy, simply break up the clumps with a fork or spoon. (See also tip.)

PELLET-FUELED GRILL

1. Preheat your grill to 250°F, using pellet flavor of your choice.

2. Spread salt evenly on a foil-lined baking tray.

3. Place salt into grill, close lid, and let smoke for about 30 minutes.

4. Remove salt from grill, and let cool to room temperature.

5. Form foil lining into a funnel and pour into a glass jar with a good sealable lid.

6. Store in a cool, dry place for as long as you like. If it gets clumpy, simply break up the clumps with a fork or spoon. (See also tip.)

TIP: BEFORE POURING SALT INTO GLASS JAR, FILL BOTTOM OF THE JAR ABOUT ¼ INCH WITH WHITE RICE. THIS HELPS TO KEEP MOISTURE OUT OF THE SALT AND REDUCES CLUMPING.

Apple

Mesquite

Hickory

• CHAPTER THREE •

APPETIZERS

BACON-WRAPPED CHORIZO AND CHEESE-STUFFED JALAPEÑO POPPERS

It's a universal truth that everything is better with bacon. Seriously, have you ever been disappointed when you spotted bacon on a dish? This is especially true for grilling. That's why when I make jalapeño poppers for my friends and family, I use a half slice of bacon to wrap these fresh-off-the-grill treats.

Filled with a blend of cheeses, chorizo, and chives, there's no resisting these classic tailgate treats. Simple to make and a guaranteed crowd pleaser, this recipe is a perfect way to try out two-zone cooking for novice grill seekers. With just enough chorizo and jalapeño to bring the heat without overpowering your palate, these poppers will make you the hit of any party, tailgate, or dinner.

So fire up the grill and get poppin'. Bet you can't eat just one!

12 large jalapeños

½ cup cream cheese, room temperature

½ cup shredded cheddar cheese

½ cup shredded jack cheese

½ cup crumbled and cooked chorizo

¼ cup finely chopped chives

1 Tbsp. BBQ rub (page 13), plus a few shakes

6 slices thin-cut bacon, cut in half

1. Cut jalapeños into a boat shape by removing between $1/8$ and $1/4$ of the pepper to create the "boat." Finely mince the portion of the pepper you cut away and remove and discard seeds and veins, but leave stems on.

2. In mixing bowl, mix together cream cheese, cheddar cheese, jack cheese, chorizo crumbles, chives, minced jalapeño, and BBQ rub.

3. Stuff jalapeño boats with equal parts of the cheese mixture. Place in freezer for 30 to 40 minutes. This step is crucial in order to allow the bacon to crisp while cooking.

4. Light grill and set up for two-zone cooking at 350°F.

5. Remove jalapeño boats from freezer and wrap each with a piece of bacon. Secure bacon with toothpick.

6. Dust bacon-wrapped boats with light coat of BBQ rub.

7. Place on grill over indirect heat. Grill for 20 minutes or until bacon is crisp and cheese is melting.

8. Remove from grill and serve hot with your favorite dipping sauce. I love these with ranch dressing.

TIP:
TRY DIPPING THESE SANDWICHES IN SOME SEEKER SAUCE (PAGE 20) FOR AN ADDED DIMENSION OF FLAVOR.

FRENCH ONION GRILLED CHEESE BITES

Cheesy, flavorful, and filling, French onion soup is one of the all-time great comfort foods. I eat it all winter and into the summer. There's only one problem: the mess. After hours of caramelizing onions, letting flavors infuse, and broiling cheese, who wants to scrub pots and pans?

I've found a way to capture the delicious beefy flavor of French onion soup without all that fuss. This recipe offers a unique twist on a comforting classic that will only *taste* like you spent hours slaving over a hot stove. Serve these sandwiches at your next party and watch how quickly they disappear. So set up your grill, sit back, and wait for your friends to beg for the recipe.

ONIONS

3 Tbsp. butter

2 Tbsp. olive oil

2 medium yellow onions, thinly sliced

2 Tbsp. Worcestershire sauce

2 Tbsp. fresh chopped parsley

1 tsp. garlic powder

½ tsp. celery salt

½ tsp. fresh ground black pepper

¼ tsp. turmeric (optional)

1½ cups beef broth

SANDWICH

4 large slices sourdough bread, or your favorite sandwich bread

4 thin slices Gruyère cheese (room temperature)

4 thin slices Swiss cheese (room temperature)

drizzle of olive oil

4 cherry tomatoes, cut in half

bamboo knot picks (or toothpicks)

1. Light grill and set up for medium-high direct heat.

2. In medium-sized frying pan over medium heat, melt butter with olive oil.

3. Add remaining ingredients for onions except the broth. Allow onions to cook down for 10 minutes.

4. Gradually add ¾ cup beef broth, mixing onions as broth reduces. When broth has completely reduced, add remaining broth and repeat. Total time should be about 30 minutes, and deep-brown-colored onions should be left without liquid.

5. Make sandwiches by layering them with Gruyère, onions, and Swiss.

6. Drizzle bread with olive oil and place on grill grate over direct heat. Grill till bread is toasted, then flip and repeat.

7. When both sides of bread are toasted and cheese is melted, remove and let cool for 5 minutes.

8. Cut diagonally into quarters. Top each quarter of sandwich with ½ a cherry tomato and skewer with bamboo knot pick or toothpick.

9. Plate and serve as finger food.

GRILLED FIG AND PROSCIUTTO FLATBREAD WITH ROSEMARY BALSAMIC GLAZE

Flatbread is a versatile dish that you can serve for a dinner party or for a family supper. Cut it into small pieces and serve as an appetizer, or devour the whole thing yourself and consider dinner sorted for the evening. It's fancy pizza for adults.

Don't let the word *fancy* fool you, however; this recipe is as easy as it is delicious. You don't even have to make the bread—I pick mine up at Trader Joe's!

Riffing on classic prosciutto pairings, this flatbread features a fig spread, goat cheese, and arugula for a taste of Italy that will make your palate sing. If you're not sure about goat cheese, consider substituting Brie, which makes for a more buttery, decadent dish. Rosemary gives a new twist to the traditional balsamic glaze, and baby arugula ensures that your greens aren't too bitter or competing with the subtle flavors of the prosciutto and cheese.

Set up your grill for indirect heat, mix the glaze, and you'll have warm, delicious flatbread for any occasion in no time.

BALSAMIC GLAZE

2 cups balsamic vinegar

1 Tbsp. unsalted butter

¾ cup brown sugar

2 sprigs rosemary

FLATBREAD

2 flatbreads (use your favorite premade breads)

8 oz. (about 12 Tbsp.) fig spread

1 cup goat cheese

6 oz. prosciutto

4 cups baby arugula

½ medium red onion, thinly sliced

1. Light grill and set up for indirect heat at 425°F.

2. For the glaze: In a saucepan over medium heat, warm balsamic vinegar and butter until butter melts. Whisk in brown sugar until sugar has fully incorporated. Then add in rosemary sprigs. Bring mixture to a low boil, reduce heat to low, and simmer uncovered until glaze reduces by half (about 20 minutes). Remove rosemary sprigs and set glaze aside.

3. As glaze simmers, coat one side of each flatbread with equal amounts of fig spread, prosciutto, and goat cheese. Place in grill over indirect heat, close lid, and cook 5–7 minutes or until bread is lightly crisp and prosciutto starts to brown.

4. Remove from grill, drizzle with balsamic glaze, and top with arugula and red onion.

5. Cut each flatbread into 4 equal-size pieces and serve hot.

GRILLED GRAPES AND ROASTED-GARLIC-INFUSED RICOTTA CROSTINI

When you think about grilling, grapes aren't generally the first thing that comes to mind. After trying this, you'll have changed your mind about that. This appetizer couldn't be simpler to make and makes the perfect addition to any party either at home or away.

I was inspired to do this by my good friend and amazing chef Andrés Dangond from The Cut restaurant in Irvine, California, who made a version of this one afternoon as we grilled together—and by grilled together, I mean he took me to school. The point here is to think outside the box. Grilling doesn't always have to be a burger or a steak . . . though I love both equally as much. Experiment and, as always, have fun!

4 cloves garlic

½ cup olive oil for mix, plus some extra for drizzle

pinch of salt

1¾ cups (15 oz.) ricotta cheese

1 tsp. cracked black pepper

2 Tbsp. balsamic vinegar

1 tsp. crushed red pepper flakes

1 Tbsp. sea salt

1 bunch seedless red grapes, about a pound (leave in bunch, do not remove) baguette or bread of your choice

6 basil leaves, finely chopped

1. Drizzle 4 cloves of garlic with olive oil, add a pinch of salt, and roast on your grill or in your oven at 350°F for 15 minutes.

2. Crush roasted garlic with fork until it becomes a paste. Mix thoroughly into ricotta cheese and cracked black pepper, and let sit. The longer this sits, the better the flavors will meld together. I shoot for at least 2 hours.

3. In mixing bowl, whisk together olive oil, balsamic vinegar, red pepper flakes, and sea salt. Add in grapes still in the bunch. Gently toss and ensure even coating on all grapes.

4. Slice bread to ½-inch slices and drizzle with olive oil.

5. Over medium-high direct heat, grill bread to achieve a nice toasted surface. Remove from heat and spread cheese mixture evenly.

6. With grapes still in the bunch, grill over high direct heat. This won't take long, only 30–40 seconds per "side." Remove from heat as grapes just start to shrivel.

7. Gently remove grapes from stems and place them on the cheese-covered bread slices.

8. Garnish with finely chopped basil.

TIP:
GENTLY SQUEEZING THE GRAPES AS YOU PLACE THEM ON THE BURRATA TOAST CAN HELP TO PREVENT A MESS WHEN BITING INTO THEM.

GRILLED STUFFED TOMATOES

I've loved tomatoes for as long as I can remember. As a kid I would literally eat them like an apple with just a little salt on them. Of course, I was also the kid that ate tomato and mayo sandwiches on Wonder bread—oh, those were the days! My love for tomatoes is still strong today. I use them as often as I can, and I experiment all the time. Without a doubt, one of my favorite ways to eat these red balls of deliciousness is to stuff and grill them. The flames really intensify the flavor, and this stuffing mix is the yin to the yang of a grilled tomato.

5 medium beefsteak tomatoes

STUFFING

5 oz. sweet Italian sausage, finely chopped

3 Tbsp. butter (the herb butter on page 15 is perfect here)

2 cloves garlic, minced (if using herb butter, use only 1 clove)

1 cup shredded Parmesan cheese

½ cup Italian bread crumbs

1 tsp. smoked salt (page 22)

¼ cup basil chiffonade (chiffonade is fancy for thinly sliced)

3 Tbsp. chopped flat-leaf parsley (set aside a dash for topping)

TOPPING

3 Tbsp. olive oil

3 Tbsp. shredded Parmesan cheese

pinch of salt

dash of divided parsley from above

1. Light grill and prepare for medium-high direct heat (350°–375°F).

2. Crumble and cook sausage in pan over medium heat. Remove cooked sausage and allow to cool, leaving the drippings in the pan.

3. Place butter and minced garlic in sausage drippings and sauté till golden brown, about 1 minute. Remove and pour entire contents of pan over sausage.

4. While sausage is cooling, remove tops from tomatoes, scoop out meat of tomatoes, and rinse off seeds. Roughly chop tomato meat and place into mixing bowl.

5. In the mixing bowl with the tomato meat, add remaining ingredients for stuffing along with the room-temperature sausage. Mix thoroughly.

6. Fill tomatoes with stuffing mix, letting it mound on top, and then top each with a drizzle of olive oil, a sprinkle of shredded Parmesan cheese, and a pinch of salt.

7. Place on grill, close lid, and let cook 10–15 minutes or until tomato skins start to split and cheese is golden brown.

8. Remove from grill, garnish with a dash of parsley, and serve while warm.

GRILLED WATERMELON WITH FETA CHEESE AND SMOKED SALT

Nothing screams summertime quite like watermelon. It was one of the few sweet treats I had as a kid. I can still remember like it was yesterday being face deep in a giant slice—juice dripping down my cheeks—and spitting the seeds in a distance competition with the other neighborhood boys. This was before the "seedless" variety was available—or at least it wasn't available in the garden my mom kept out back.

Anyway, having celebrated several anniversaries of my twenty-ninth birthday, it doesn't seem quite as appropriate to bury my face in the slices and spit the seeds like I used to. (Lame, right?) But that doesn't mean I don't still love me some watermelon, and grilling it with feta makes even a basic guy like me look extra.

1 small seedless watermelon

¼ cup olive oil

2 Tbsp. smoked salt (page 22)

½ cup feta cheese

¼ cup fresh basil leaves

1 Tbsp. red pepper flakes (optional)

1. Light grill and set up for direct cooking at medium-high heat.

2. Leaving the rind on, cut watermelon into 1-inch-thick slices, then cut those slices into quarters and remove any seeds. Don't attempt to do these as "steaks" because they will fall apart on the grill. I know this from experience. Lightly brush both sides of each watermelon quarter with olive oil, and season with smoked salt.

3. Grill watermelon quarters about 1 minute on each side or until grill marks appear.

4. Place watermelon on a serving plate. Top with feta cheese, basil, and a pinch of red pepper flakes, if desired. Serve immediately.

HICKORY-SMOKED JACK CHEESE MOINK BALLS

First things first: There is no moink animal. Don't ask for it at your local butcher shop. You'll get a weird look. Moink balls get their name from the sounds the components make: beef (moo) and pork (oink). Put them together and you get a combination that's hard to beat.

Glazed with a pepper jelly and wrapped in bacon (because if you can't wrap it in bacon, what's the point?), these appetizers are going to go fast at your next cookout. I once watched a friend devour thirteen of these hearty appetizers in one sitting, and I legit thought he was going to burst, so be sure to account for those with big appetites when you're making them.

I've added a twist on the typical moink recipe by stuffing these delicious concoctions with cheese. Why? Because I like cheese. ("I like cheese" is my default response to any question I can't answer. Try it out sometime. It's a surprisingly good answer for many of life's questions, and certainly a topic changer when you're in a pinch.)

1 Tbsp. olive oil

1 medium jalapeño, finely seeded, deveined, and diced (optional)

¼ cup diced sweet onion

2 cloves garlic, freshly minced

½ lb. ground beef, at least 20 percent fat

½ lb. pork sausage

½ cup bread crumbs

1 large egg, lightly beaten

2 Tbsp. BBQ rub (page 13) or your favorite rub, plus a few shakes

8 (½-inch) cubes pepper jack cheese

8 slices thin-cut bacon, cut in half

¾ cup pepper jelly

1. Heat oil in small sauté pan, adding jalapeño, onion, and garlic. Sauté for 3 minutes or until onions become translucent. Set aside.

2. In mixing bowl, add ground beef, sausage, breadcrumbs, egg, BBQ rub, and sauté mix. Mix thoroughly and divide into 8 equal portions.

3. Lightly form each portion into a ball. Insert cheese cube into center of each ball, ensuring that the meat "seals" the cheese all around.

4. Place balls in freezer for 30–40 minutes. This step is critical in order for the bacon to crisp during the cooking process. If bacon and meatballs are the same temperature when they go on the grill, the meatball will be done before the bacon is crisp.

5. Light grill and set up for indirect heat. Add wood chunks. Place drip pan under cooking area to catch bacon grease and avoid the mess in your grill. Maintain grill temperature at 325°F.

6. Wrap each ball with 2 half slices of bacon. By cutting the bacon in half, the balls can be wrapped completely by wrapping the first half of the slice in a north-south direction and the second half in an east-west direction on the ball. Secure bacon with toothpick.

TIP:
WARMING THE JELLY IN THE MICROWAVE FOR 30 SECONDS MAKES IT MUCH EASIER TO GLAZE.

7. Lightly dusk moink balls with a few shakes of the BBQ rub.

8. Place on grill on the indirect heat side, close lid, and let cook for 20 minutes. Check internal temperature (we're looking for 145°–150°F internal temperature).

9. Once the balls have reached a sufficient internal temperature, glaze moink balls with pepper jelly. Place back on grill, close lid, and allow to cook for another 5 minutes or until internal temperature is 160°F, which is safe for ground pork.

10. Remove from grill and serve hot.

PROSCIUTTO BRIE BITES WITH FIG JAM

What's better than bringing an impressive dish to the table and basking in the compliments of friends and family? It's bringing that impressive dish to the table, soaking up all those compliments, and knowing that it was incredibly easy to make.

This is that dish. Beautiful, simple, and always the first to go at any party, prosciutto Brie bites with fig jam is the holy grail of shareable appetizers. It'll be the star of the show whether you're serving it at a formal dinner party or a neighborhood get-together. The salty, crisp prosciutto is balanced by the gooey sweetness of the jam and the creamy texture of the cheese. This is a decadent dish, and you will want to devour it whole. (I've done it a few times, and I don't regret it.)

My only caution is this: Hold back the crowd for a few minutes. The fig jam and cheese are incredibly hot fresh off the grill, and nothing ruins a dinner party faster than guests burning their fingers.

12 Brie wheels (I use Trader Joe's 0.9-oz. mini Brie bites)

1 jar fig spread

12 slices prosciutto

1. Light grill and set up for two-zone heat at 250°F.

2. Unwrap the Brie bites and add a dollop of the fig jam to the top of each.

3. Wrap each Brie wheel topped with fig spread with one piece of prosciutto. Wrap tightly, tucking the prosciutto under the bottom of the wheel.

4. Place each bite over direct heat, tucked side down, and grill for 1 to 2 minutes.

5. Flip each wheel and grill for an additional 1 to 2 minutes until prosciutto starts to brown and crisp.

6. Move wheels to indirect heat, close lid, and cook additional 5 minutes.

7. Remove from grill and serve immediately.

ROASTED RANCH CORN SALSA

This is a great summertime dish that can be used for either a dip with some tortilla chips or as a stand-alone side dish. I like making this salsa in the summer because that's when I can get the super fresh ingredients I love, either from my garden or from a local farmers market (and I love to buy local when possible). Not only is it a match made in heaven for either grilled chicken or glazed salmon, it's an awesome condiment for those hot dogs that are at every summer barbecue. Admittedly, despite all of the incredible meals I've had over the years, hot dogs remain one of my all-time favorites. Don't judge.

8 ears fresh sweet corn

2 Tbsp. salt (for water)

3 green onions, finely sliced

2 jalapeños, seeded and deveined (if you want to add some heat to this, you can leave the seeds in one or both peppers)

1 large tomato, diced with seeds removed

1 cup roughly chopped and loosely packed cilantro

½ medium red onion, diced

½ red bell pepper, diced

½ cup feta cheese

¼ cup olive oil

1-oz. package ranch dip mix

3 Tbsp. apple cider vinegar

2 Tbsp. smoked salt (page 22), or to taste

2 Tbsp. white sugar

1. Peel back husks of corn and remove and discard all the silk (the fine hair-like strands inside the husk near the corn). This is sort of messy, so do it over the garbage or an old newspaper to help clean up.

2. Place corn, husks peeled back, into large bowl of water mixed with 2 tablespoons of salt; let soak 10–15 minutes.

3. Light grill and set up for indirect heat at 325°F.

4. Remove corn from bowl, shake off excess water, and return the husks back up around the corn. This is going to protect the corn from burning and will partially steam the corn in the salt water contained within the husk.

5. Place corn on the indirect heat side of the grill for about 15 minutes.

6. Remove corn and peel back husks. (Careful! They'll be hot.) Place corn over direct heat, turning as some of the kernels begin to brown. You don't want all of them to char, just about 25 percent or so to add some texture and multiple flavor profiles to the dish.

7. When all sides are cooked, remove from grill. Cut corn off cob into a large mixing bowl. Combine remaining ingredients and mix thoroughly.

SWEET HEAT BACON-WRAPPED PLANTAINS

You may have noticed a certain ingredient keeps popping up in my recipes. I've long known that bacon is a perfect food, and I just want to make sure you know it too. It's my belief that adding bacon to just about anything is an improvement, and I'll prove it here. (Not to mention that bacon is essentially the duct tape of the culinary world and helps to keep things together!)

Grilled plantains are delicious and sweet. Pairing them with savory bacon takes this dish to a whole new level. Plantains also aren't a common appetizer in the United States, so be prepared for everyone to ask for the recipe. Just dog-ear the page for quick reference.

The cayenne pepper adds a little heat, but for those who like life on the mild side, try substituting some of my smoked salts for the cayenne. This is also a great basic recipe for novice grillers. So fire up the grill and master some fundamentals while making a sweet and savory appetizer that's sure to impress.

2 large medium-ripe plantains

8 slices of thin-cut bacon, cut in half crosswise

2 Tbsp. honey

1 Tbsp. brown sugar

2 tsp. cayenne pepper or smoked salt (page 22)

1. Light grill and set up for indirect heat at 375°–400°F.

2. Peel plantains and cut them into quarters lengthwise, then cut the quarters in half crosswise.

3. Wrap each piece of plantain with a half slice of bacon and secure with small skewer or toothpick.

4. Baste each piece of bacon-wrapped plantain with a very light coat of honey, then dust with brown sugar and cayenne pepper (or salt).

5. Place on grill over indirect heat and close lid. Cook till bacon is crispy (about 30 minutes).

6. Remove from grill and serve.

CHAPTER FOUR

BEEF

BBQ BEEF TIPS WITH GRILLED GARLIC GREEN BEANS

The term "beef tips" means different things to different people. Most commonly beef tips are either the tip of a sirloin or the tips of a loin. Not big enough to be cut into steaks, tips are often used in kebabs or cooked in a slow cooker as stew meat. If you buy a whole loin and cut your own steaks—filet is much cheaper that way—this is a great way to make use of those tips. Sirloin tips, which are less expensive, can still be just as flavorful (albeit not as tender).

As with any dish, the marinade can make or break it. With the right marinade, the flavor of the dish will be incredible. I'm lucky to have a wonderful butcher, Carlo Crocetti, who offers pre-marinated meats. If you don't have pre-marinated meats, use this simple and easy way to do it yourself. The other benefit of making your own marinade? It opens up a world of possibilities and allows for creativity.

Because beef tips are small, they cook quickly. This is a great meal to prep the night before and grill on a busy weekday evening. Grilling the beans as well gives them a bit of char that adds to the flavor. They sure beat the mushy green beans I had to force myself to eat through childhood.

Fast, delicious, and budget friendly, this recipe should be your go-to for a feast-in-a-flash weeknight meal.

1.5-2 lb. beef tips

BEEF MARINADE

1 cup BBQ sauce

½ cup Worcestershire sauce

¼ cup red wine vinegar

¼ cup olive oil

4 cloves garlic, minced

1 Tbsp. chopped rosemary

1 tsp. fresh ground pepper

BEANS

1 lb. green beans, washed and trimmed

¼ cup olive oil

1 tsp. sea salt

1 tsp. garlic powder

½ tsp. crushed red pepper flakes

1. Combine beef marinade ingredients into mixing bowl and whisk together.
2. Place beef tips in sealable plastic bag along with marinade. Squeeze excess air from bag, seal, and place in refrigerator for 4–6 hours, or overnight.
3. Light grill and set up for medium-high direct heat.
4. Toss beans with olive oil to coat thoroughly. Then add in sea salt, garlic powder, and red pepper flakes, and toss to evenly distribute.
5. Place grill pan on one side of grill over direct heat. Add beans to the pan. Turn beans every 90 seconds. After 3–5 minutes, place beef on other side of grill over direct heat.
6. Turn steak tips occasionally for 5–7 minutes or until done.
7. Remove both beef and green beans from grill, plate, and serve immediately.

BOSTON STRIP STEAK WITH ROASTED GARLIC AND BLUE CHEESE BUTTER

This steak is one of the best-kept secrets among grillers. It was made famous by old-world craftsman butcher Carlo Crocetti, who trademarked the cut in 2014. As the name suggests, Carlo is from Boston, where he's a fourth-generation butcher.

Because various cuts of meat go by different names in different regions of the country, let me break down what exactly a Boston strip steak is. The steak is a cross-cut from the bottom sirloin flap, and it packs one of the most intense beef flavors you'll come across. From a value perspective, I don't know that there's a better cut of beef. It's well marbled, tender, inexpensive, and delicious.

A robust cut of beef, this steak cooks best when done simply—a little salt is all that's needed. But if you add my garlic and blue cheese butter, this will be a dish you'll want to make every night.

2 tsp. olive oil

1 large Vidalia onion, sliced

1 tsp. Worcestershire sauce

2 to 4 (8-oz.) Boston strip steaks

½ tsp. sea salt per steak

1 Tbsp. roasted garlic and blue cheese butter (page 14) per steak

1. Light grill and set up for high direct heat.

2. In medium-sized sauté pan, heat olive oil over medium-high heat. Sauté onions, adding Worcestershire sauce after onions have cooked for 5 minutes.

3. Prepare each steak by sprinkling each with ½ teaspoon of sea salt.

4. Place steaks on hot grill directly over heat. Grill for 2 minutes, rotate 90 degrees, and grill for an additional 2 minutes.

5. Flip steak and repeat step 4, removing from grill when internal temperature reaches 125°F (for medium-rare).

6. Serve over sautéed onions, and top with 1 tablespoon of roasted garlic and blue cheese butter.

BRAZILIAN ROTISSERIE PICANHA

If you frequent Brazilian steakhouses, you know they start out by offering you generally less-expensive cuts of meat, like chicken and sausage, in the hopes you'll fill up on them. Savvy customers hold out for the filet and feast on expensive quality cuts. But here's a little secret to remember the next time you're headed to a Brazilian steakhouse: What you should be holding out for is the picanha.

Picanha is not a well-known piece of beef in the United States. In Brazil, however, it is prized for good reason: it's simple to cook and delicious. The picanha is a sirloin cap (also known as a rump cover, rump cap, or coulotte). The meat itself is pretty lean with very little intermuscular fat, but it is cut with the thick fat cap left on, which allows it to baste in its own juices while it spins. Unlike other cuts of meat, the end cap is often the tastiest—so keep that tidbit to yourself and let everyone think you're selfless!

If you don't want the hassle of the red card–green card game at the Brazilian steakhouse, make picanha yourself and have a ton of fun in the process. There's something so primal about watching your dinner spin on a rotisserie over a fire. The whole family can join in the fun of this roast!

1 (approx. 3 lb.) top sirloin cap (aka picanha)

2 Tbsp. olive oil

3 cloves fresh garlic, minced

2 Tbsp. rosemary salt (page 19)

1. Light grill and set up for rotisserie cooking, coals positioned under the rotisserie. This will result in an occasional flare up, but don't sweat it—that's part of the authentic cooking process. The rendered fat dripping into the fire will also add flavor to the meat.

2. Cut the cap steak into 5 or 6 individual thick steaks. Rub each steak with olive oil and dust with minced garlic and rosemary salt.

3. Shape each steak into a semicircle, with the thick fat layer forming the outside, curved edge of the circle, and skewer onto rotisserie rod so it maintains that C shape. The thick layer of fat will add in basting the meat as it spins and prevent the otherwise lean meat from drying out during the cooking process.

4. Place rotisserie on grill, high above coals, and cook about 20 minutes or until desired level of doneness.

5. Remove from grill, let rest for 5 minutes, and slice directly from skewer to serve.

TIP:
CUTTING THIS STEAK INTO CUBES AND USING THE SAME MARINADE MAKES FOR DELICIOUS AND COLORFUL KEBABS.

EN FUEGO FLAP STEAK

Flap meat might just be the *most* underrated cut of meat. It's likely your friends and family have never heard of it. Visually, it looks similar to hanger steak, but the two cuts of meat come from different parts of the steer. The flap steak is from the bottom sirloin, and in the northwest United States it's sometimes called sirloin tip. Hanger, on the other hand, comes from the plate, or belly, of the steer. While hanger is more expensive, I'm going to prove to you that flap steak is just as flavorful and fun to cook.

In contrast to its modest price, flap steak boasts exceptional flavor and does extremely well in a marinade due to its porous texture. Over my years of grilling, I developed a marinade for it that has a heavy Asian influence. As I said, I like a bit of heat, but only if it doesn't get in the way of flavor. I wouldn't call this marinade unreasonably hot, but it will clear your sinuses for sure!

There are two very important things to remember when grilling and serving flap steak: First, this steak is best served at a medium degree of doneness; any more and it will get a bit tough. Second, always cut it across the grain to serve or it will have a stringy texture.

2 lbs. flap steak (you can also use skirt steak, hanger steak, or pork loin)

MARINADE

¾ cup soy sauce

½ cup rice vinegar

½ cup honey

½ cup roughly chopped cilantro

¼ cup brown sugar

3 Tbsp. sriracha sauce

3 Tbsp. chopped ginger

2 Tbsp. fish sauce

1 Tbsp. crushed red pepper flakes

1 Tbsp. Dijon mustard

3 cloves garlic, chopped

2 green onions, thinly sliced (use the whole onion)

1 medium jalapeño, sliced

1. Combine all marinade ingredients in a large mixing bowl and whisk together.
2. Cut steaks into 2-inch strips, cutting with the grain, and place into sealable bag. Cutting them with the grain here allows you to cut across the grain when you serve.
3. Set aside ½ cup of the marinade for dipping sauce. Pour remaining marinade over steak, ensuring the entire surface of the meat is covered. Squeeze excess air from bag before sealing.
4. Place bag on a plate to catch any leaks and place in refrigerator 4–6 hours, flipping every hour or so to ensure even marinating.
5. Remove steaks from marinade and pat dry. The flavor has already infused into the meat, and the drier the steaks are when you place them on the grill, the better they will sear. Additionally, the high sugar content of this marinade will burn over open fire. Let steaks warm up to room temperature for about 30 minutes while you light your grill.
6. Light grill and prepare for direct cooking.
7. Place steaks directly over heat and grill for about 5 minutes per side.

GRILLED FLANK STEAK WITH JALAPEÑO CHIMICHURRI

Chimichurri is one of those all-purpose sauces that brighten just about anything. On beef, chicken, or seafood, chimichurri packs a flavorful punch that will make your mouth water. I've never tried it on ice cream, but I'm willing to bet it wouldn't be bad there either! One of my favorite proteins to pair with chimichurri is flank steak, which is easy to cook and incredibly tasty. You can also use flank steak and chimichurri for a great twist on tacos or fajitas.

To get the most out of my chimichurri, I like to start with the freshest ingredients possible. That means hitting up the local farmers market in the summer and buying as much as I can locally. There are two benefits to this: First, farm-fresh herbs make for the brightest and most flavorful chimichurri. Second, the more you go to the farmers market, the better you get to know your local vendors. If you make friends with them, some may set aside their best produce for you each week.

One of the most diverse sauces in any griller's arsenal, chimichurri is a fast, delicious way to put a tangy twist on typical proteins.

MEAT

1 flank steak, roughly 1.5 to 2 lb. trimmed

olive oil (enough for a light coat)

1 Tbsp. salt, preferably hickory smoked salt (page 22), but sea salt works well also

CHIMICHURRI SAUCE

3 cloves garlic, finely minced

1 shallot, finely chopped

1 red jalapeño, seeded and finely chopped

2 Tbsp. finely chopped chives

¾ cup finely chopped fresh cilantro

¾ cup finely chopped fresh flat-leaf parsley

¾ cup extra-virgin olive oil

1½ Tbsp. red wine vinegar

3 tsp. kosher salt (or to taste)

1 tsp. lemon juice

1. Light grill and prepare for direct heat. You'll want your grill as hot as possible for this cut of meat. This means if you're using a charcoal grill, get the coals as close to the grate as possible. If using a gas grill, set the burner to maximum and let the grate get as hot as possible.

2. While grill is heating up, add garlic, shallot, jalapeño, chives, cilantro, and parsley to a bowl. Toss gently until combined.

3. In the same bowl, whisk in olive oil, red wine vinegar, salt, and lemon juice. Set aside.

4. Pat steak dry of any moisture and lightly coat with olive oil. Lightly season meat with salt. Because you're using this incredible chimichurri, you don't want to overdo the seasoning on the meat.

5. Place meat on grate over direct heat and let it cook 3 minutes per side. This will produce a perfect char and a medium-rare center that suits the cut of meat best. More than medium-rare and this cut tends to get a bit tough. Don't move the steak once it's on the grate until you're ready to turn it.

6. Remove from grill and let rest 5 minutes.

7. Slice and serve with chimichurri.

TIP:
GETTING THIS CUT OF MEAT COMPLETELY DRY IS KEY FOR HOT AND FAST COOKING AND FOR GETTING THE RIGHT CRUST. IF THE MEAT HAS ANY MOISTURE ON IT, IT WILL STEAM THE STEAK AND PREVENT THAT CRUST FROM FORMING UNTIL THE MOISTURE HAS EVAPORATED, AND BY THAT TIME THE INSIDE WILL BE OVERCOOKED.

TIP:
THE CHIMICHURRI IS BEST MADE 1–2 HOURS BEFORE SERVING IF POSSIBLE, ALLOWING THE FLAVORS TO MELD TOGETHER.

MARINATED LONDON BROIL

London broil is often overlooked in butcher shops and meat departments. It has a reputation for being tough and a bit flavorless. But cooked correctly, this cheap cut can become fit for a king.

As with so many things in life, preparation is key to cooking London broil. With this thick cut, marinating is a good idea to help tenderize the meat. Crosshatch both sides of the meat (don't cut deeper than ¼ inch) before you put it in the marinade; the crosshatching lets the marinade sink in while helping the meat evenly cook during the grilling process. After marinating, let the meat reach room temperature, and then use the high direct heat grilling method to sear in flavor and enhance the char. Don't take this cut warmer than medium rare, however, or you risk getting a tough finish on your food.

Served thinly sliced with a simple au jus or my chipotle aioli (page 21), London broil is a budget-friendly way to create a feast for friends.

2-lb. London broil

MARINADE

½ cup soy sauce

2 Tbsp. balsamic vinegar

2 Tbsp. Dijon mustard

4 cloves garlic, minced

2 Tbsp. olive oil

3 sprigs fresh rosemary

1 tsp. coarsely ground black pepper

1. Combine all marinade ingredients in mixing bowl and whisk together.

2. Using a sharp knife, cut a diamond, or crosshatch, pattern into each side of the meat, only cutting about ¼ inch deep. This will allow the marinade to penetrate the meat deeper in a shorter amount of time.

3. Place meat in sealable plastic bag and cover with marinade. Place in refrigerator for 2 hours.

4. After 2 hours, remove from refrigerator and allow to come up to room temperature for 1 hour.

5. Light grill and prepare for high direct heat.

6. Remove meat from marinade and pat dry with paper towel. Place directly over high heat. Let cook for 2 minutes, rotate 90 degrees, and allow to cook for another 2 minutes.

7. Flip meat and repeat step six.

8. Remove from grill when internal temperature reaches 125°F. Tent with foil and let rest for 5 minutes before slicing.

9. Serve with chipotle aioli (page 21).

TIP:
LONDON BROIL IS OFTEN ON SALE FOR DOLLARS ON THE POUND. WHEN YOU FIND ONE OF THESE SALES, STOCK UP AND FREEZE WHAT YOU DON'T COOK. THIS IS A CUT OF MEAT THAT THAWS WELL!

STRIP STEAK WITH COMPOUND HERB BUTTER

Sometimes grilling can seem intimidating. That's why there's no better place to start than a simple, flavorful steak. With few ingredients and only a handful of steps, this is a great recipe to warm up your grilling skills.

The strip steak (also known as New York strip, Kansas City strip, or strip loin steak) is cut from the short loin of the steer. Because that's a muscle that doesn't get a lot of workout on a cow, it's exceptionally tender. It falls somewhere between a filet and a rib eye for fat content, meaning this is a steak that pleases most palates. Strip steaks are also uniform in shape, which makes this one of the easiest cuts of meat to cook properly on a grill.

Strip steaks are usually thick-cut, so using the reverse-sear technique described here will help ensure that your meat is evenly done. Adding my compound herb butter will make it look like you toiled for hours over this impressive dish. As with all things, it's better to work smart than hard. Don't worry, I won't tell anyone how easy dinner was tonight!

2 to 4 (14-oz. each) strip steaks, about 2 inches thick

½ tsp. olive oil per steak

½ tsp. smoked salt (page 22) per steak

1 Tbsp. compound herb butter (page 15) per steak

1. Allow steaks to warm up to room temperature.
2. Light grill and set up for two-zone heat at 225°F.
3. Rub steaks with olive oil and dust with smoked salt.
4. Place steaks on grill over indirect heat, close lid, and allow steaks to reach an internal temperature of 125°F (approximately 40 minutes).
5. Remove steaks. While steaks rest, stoke the direct heat by either cranking up the knob (on a gas grill) or adding hot coals (to a charcoal grill). Get direct heat area as hot as possible—700°F plus is desired.
6. Once grill is ready, place steak directly over direct heat, turning every 30 seconds for a total of about 5 minutes or until desired level of overall crust has built up on the steaks.
7. Remove steak from direct heat and let rest for 7–10 minutes. Top with herb butter and serve.

SIMPLY GRILLED PORTERHOUSE

Porterhouse is often thought of as the king of steaks. I know some tomahawk rib eye enthusiasts who would certainly disagree, but let's focus on porterhouses instead of all that drama.

The porterhouse is two prime cuts of meat on the same bone. On one side of the bone lies the New York strip, and on the other lies filet mignon. It's a substantial and delicious cut of meat, one that needs to be cooked carefully. Porterhouses are usually big and thick, meaning that the reverse-sear method of cooking is the best way to ensure the perfect doneness. It's also important you remember that the fat content differs between the strip and filet sides of the steak. Be sure to keep the strip side of the porterhouse toward the heat, with the filet side as far from the heat source as possible so it doesn't overcook or dry out.

Beyond the excellent flavor, porterhouse is one of the greatest steaks available because it can also be made into an excellent family-style meal. Slice up the strip and filet sides to offer your friends and family their choice of lean or not-so-lean pieces of meat. Want to pair this with the perfect side? Try my parmesan potatoes on page 136.

1 (32-oz.) porterhouse steak

1 Tbsp. olive oil

1½ tsp. smoked salt (page 22)

1. Light grill and set up for two-zone heat at 225°F.
2. Rub steak with olive oil and smoked salt.
3. Place steak over indirect heat, strip side toward heat source, and close the lid. Allow to cook until internal temperature reaches 125°F (about 45 minutes).
4. Remove steak. While steak rests, stoke the direct heat by either cranking up the knob (on a gas grill) or adding hot coals (to a charcoal grill). Get direct heat area as hot as possible—700°F plus is desired.
5. Once grill is ready, place steak directly over direct heat, turning every 30 seconds for a total of about 5 minutes or until desired level of overall crust has built up on the steak.
6. Remove from grill and let rest for 7 minutes before slicing and serving.

SMOKED AND SEARED TRI-TIP WITH CREAMY HORSERADISH

Tri-tip is one of those overlooked cuts of meat that's excellent for tailgating or cookouts. It's inexpensive, large, and—when cooked right—full of bold beef flavor. This is a cut of beef that's strong enough to stand up to any seasoning without getting overwhelmed.

I recommend my BBQ rub as a good starter for tri-tip dishes, but feel free to experiment to find the one that works best for you. If you're looking for a unique flavor to imbue into your tri-tip, try adding oak, hickory, or mesquite chunks to your grill.

The biggest secret to cooking the perfect tri-tip is to let it rest. Extended rest time works best for this cut, as it's thick and juicy. Without proper rest, the tri-tip juices will run everywhere when it's cut, and you'll be left with a mess to clean and a dry cut of meat. But if you're patient, rest it, and slice across the grain, tri-tip will be the star of your next cookout.

1 (2-lb.) tri-tip

1 Tbsp. olive oil

2 tsp. BBQ rub (page 13) or your favorite BBQ rub

HORSERADISH SAUCE

¼ cup pure horseradish

1 cup sour cream

1 tsp. fresh ground pepper

TIP:
FOR HEAT SEEKERS, DOUBLE THE HORSERADISH AMOUNT IN THIS RECIPE.

1. Light grill and set up for two-zone heat at 225°F.

2. Strain horseradish by placing it on a folded-over paper towel and wringing out the water over a sink. Without this step, the mixture will be watery.

3. In medium mixing bowl, add strained horseradish, sour cream, and ground pepper. Mix thoroughly. Place in refrigerator.

4. Rub tri-tip with olive oil and lightly dust with BBQ rub.

5. Place tri-tip on grill over indirect heat, adding 1 or 2 wood chunks to the hot coals. For a gas grill, add a pellet tube.

6. Allow to smoke to an internal temperature of 125°F.

7. Remove meat and let rest while stoking the direct heat by either cranking up the knob (on a gas grill) or adding hot coals (to a charcoal grill). Get direct heat area as hot as possible—700°F plus is desired.

8. Place meat over direct heat, turning every 30 seconds for a total of about 5 minutes or until desired level of overall crust has built up on the tri-tip.

9. Remove from grill, tent with foil, and let rest 20 minutes. Slice across the grain of the meat, and serve with horseradish sauce.

SMOKED MEAT LOAF

When I was growing up, I thought my mother was a bit of a meat loaf magician. That woman could work wonders with ground meat, creating loaves of just about any protein imaginable and serving them up regularly on the family dinner table.

About three or four years ago, I decided to take the meat loaf out of the oven and put it onto the grill. I smoked it, thinking it would be a healthier version of my favorite childhood dish because it wouldn't be sitting in a pan of its own grease anymore. Now, I know—as the guy who's told you to wrap just about everything in this book in bacon or stuff it with cheese—I'm not exactly the most credible health expert. Still, even if you don't believe this is the healthier meat loaf recipe of your dreams, you can't argue with the flavor. Try this smoke-enhanced version of the American staple and see if you ever go back to the oven again.

2 Tbsp. olive oil

1 medium sweet onion, chopped

1/2 cup chopped celery

1/4 cup diced red bell pepper

1/4 cup diced yellow bell pepper

5 slices white bread

½ cup buttermilk

1 package dried onion soup mix

1.5 lb. ground beef (80/20)

1 lb. ground Italian sausage

2 Tbsp. Worcestershire sauce

1½ cups BBQ sauce, divided in half

2 large eggs

1. Heat olive oil in a pan over medium heat and sauté the chopped onion, celery, and peppers for about 5 minutes or until onions become translucent. Remove and set aside.

2. Tear the bread into small chunks and soak in buttermilk. These soaked pieces will keep your meat loaf moist as it cooks because, let's face it, there's not much worse than a dry meat loaf.

3. In large mixing bowl, combine soup mix with ground beef and sausage. Mix by hand until it's thoroughly incorporated.

4. Add to the meat mixture the sautéed ingredients, soaked bread chunks, Worcestershire sauce, ³⁄₄ cup of the BBQ sauce, and eggs (fold these in).

5. On a sheet of tinfoil, form the mixture into a loaf roughly 6 in. long, 4 in. wide, and 2 in. thick. Place in the freezer for about 15 minutes, just to firm it up.

6. Light grill and set up for indirect heat at 250°F, adding a few chunks of mild wood for smoke. I use apple or pecan for this. If you're using a gas grill, be sure you use a smoke tube.

7. Transfer chilled meat loaf from tinfoil to cooling rack, and place rack into preheated grill.

8. When the internal temperature of your loaf gets to 150°F, glaze it with remaining BBQ sauce and crank grill temperature up to 350°F. Continue cooking for about 10 minutes. This temperature allows the sauce to set up and get that beautiful color.

9. Remove from grill when the meat loaf temperature reaches 160°F internal temperature.

TIP:
FOR AN ADDED KICK, LIGHTLY DUST THE FINISHED LOAF WITH BBQ RUB (PAGE 13).

• CHAPTER FIVE •

POULTRY

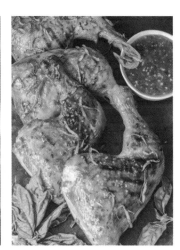

CHICKEN SATAY WITH THAI PEANUT SAUCE

Satay originates in Southwest Asia and is similar to what many of us would call a kebab. It's made by cutting meat into thin strips or small chunks and threading them onto wooden skewers called satay sticks. The meat is often marinated but not always; I prefer to keep the seasoning light because the peanut sauce packs a ton of flavor.

The meat is grilled over direct heat. Because it isn't thickly cut, it will cook fast, get a nice char, and be filled with flavor via the Maillard reaction in the process. This sauce differs from those boring peanut sauces that generally taste like nothing more than a melted scoop of peanut butter. I've developed this version to avoid the ho-hum standard taste, incorporating interesting flavors like fish sauce to liven up the peanut butter and complement the smoky skewers.

3 large boneless skinless chicken breasts or 6 boneless skinless thighs

satay sticks

THAI PEANUT SAUCE

1 cup creamy peanut butter

¾ cup coconut milk

3 Tbsp. soy sauce

3 Tbsp. fresh lime juice

3 Tbsp. brown sugar

2 Tbsp. sesame oil

2 tsp. crushed red pepper flakes

1 Tbsp. fish sauce

1 Tbsp. sriracha sauce

1 (3-in.) piece of ginger, peeled and diced

2 cloves garlic, minced

¼ cup chopped cilantro

1. Light grill and prepare for direct grilling over medium heat.

2. Cut chicken into 1.5-inch squares and place onto satay sticks. Lightly season with salt.

3. Combine all ingredients for sauce except the cilantro into a saucepan.

4. Place saucepan over medium heat, mix ingredients together using a whisk, and let simmer for 5 minutes.

5. Once ingredients have melded together, use either a blender or an immersion blender to blend until smooth.

6. Pour into bowl and top with cilantro.

7. Spray chicken with nonstick cooking spray and place directly over medium heat on grill. Because the chicken is cut into small pieces, it will cook rather quickly, about 3 to 4 minutes per side. But don't risk undercooked chicken. Ensure internal temperature meets minimum requirements of 165° Fahrenheit.

8. Remove from grill. Serve with sauce and cilantro.

TIP:
THIS CAN ALSO BE DONE
WITH PORK SATAY.
ANY LEFTOVER SAUCE IS
EXCELLENT OVER PASTA.

CITRUS ROASTED DUCK

Duck is one of those foods most people only order at a restaurant. To be honest, I'm not sure why more people don't make it at home, though I suspect it's just because it isn't as readily available at most grocery stores as chicken or beef. My issue with restaurant duck is that it's generally topped with some extra sweet sauce, which takes away from the duck flavor itself. I started using this recipe some time ago after I found duck on the cheap after a holiday and bought a dozen and a half of them for experimenting. The fact that I didn't have near the freezer space that I thought I did when buying them aided in the rapid duck recipe experimentation, but I digress. The citrus in the cavity provides just a hint of sweetness while the rub on the skin gives a bit more of a savory flavor to the crispy skin.

Important Note: I eat duck well below the USDA recommendation of 165°F—which I find to be about as appetizing as an old catcher's mitt. But do so at your own risk.

1 (5-lb.) duck

1 Tbsp. poultry rub (page 17)

1 Tbsp. olive oil

½ medium onion

1 lemon, sliced

1 orange, sliced

1 lime, sliced

4 whole garlic cloves

2 sprigs fresh rosemary

2 sprigs fresh thyme

1. Light grill and set for indirect heat, establish temperature at 425°F.

2. Rinse duck under cold water, remove any "extras" that may come with the duck from the cavity and discard. Pat dry, inside and out, with a paper towel.

3. Stuff cavity of duck with onion, lemon, orange, lime, garlic, rosemary, and thyme.

4. Coat surface of duck with olive oil and dust entire surface with poultry rub.

5. Place the duck breast-side up on a cooling rack situated inside of a roasting pan. Put on the grill and close lid for 15 minutes in order to brown the skin slightly.

6. Reduce the temperature of your grill to 325°F and roast for 30 minutes with lid closed. Open lid and, using a basting bulb, baste the duck with the drippings collected in the roasting pan.

7. Close lid, roast for additional 30 minutes or until internal temperature reaches 135°F for medium-rare duck (the USDA recommendation is 165°F).

8. Remove from grill, let rest for 10 minutes before carving.

GRILLED CHICKEN FAJITAS

People tend to think of chicken fajitas as an indoor recipe, but grilling the chicken is a surefire way to kick up the flavor. Grilling also lends a smoky flavor to classic fajita veggies. The rub for these fajitas is a versatile blend of savory, spicy flavors that you'll find yourself putting on all kinds of meats. But the real selling point for grilling your fajitas? Tortillas. If you've never had a grilled tortilla, put this book down, run to the grocery store, and be sure to thank me once you've tried one. You'll never eat a regular tortilla again.

You will need a grill pan for this recipe. It's an essential tool for all grillers; it's indispensable when grilling shrimp, spaghetti, or any other delicate item. You can find inexpensive versions online.

Quick, delicious, and inexpensive, these fajitas are a family dish you'll swear by.

CHICKEN

¼ cup olive oil, divided

juice from 1 lime

3 large boneless skinless chicken breasts, butterflied

1 each red, yellow, and orange peppers

1 medium Vidalia onion

a pinch of salt

12 small soft flour tortillas

SEASONING

1½ Tbsp. chili powder

2 tsp. ground cumin

2 tsp. kosher salt

2 tsp. smoked paprika

1 tsp. ground cinnamon

1 tsp. onion powder

1 tsp. garlic powder

1 tsp. cayenne pepper

½ tsp. white sugar

zest from 1 lime

1. Light grill and set up for medium-high direct heat.
2. Combine all the seasoning ingredients into small bowl and whisk together.
3. Whisk 2 tablespoons olive oil and the lime juice together in medium mixing bowl. Add butterflied chicken breasts. Toss to evenly coat.
4. Evenly sprinkle seasoning on both sides of chicken, ensuring uniform coverage.
5. Thinly slice peppers and onion.
6. In a large mixing bowl, toss sliced vegetables with remaining 2 tablespoons of olive oil and a pinch of salt.
7. Using a grill basket, grill vegetables over direct heat until soft and slightly charred. To prevent burning, turn veggies often as they cook.
8. As veggies near completion, place seasoned chicken on grill over direct heat. Turn every 90 seconds until done.
9. Remove both meat and vegetables from the grill, slice chicken into thin strips, and keep warm.
10. Toss flour tortillas on grill for 15 to 30 seconds per side, just to warm them up and slightly toast them. Don't cook them to the point that they are no longer flexible.
11. Serve hot with toppings of your choice: cheese, fresh limes, sour cream, cilantro, and so on.

GRILLED CRISPY HOT WINGS

When you think of chicken wings, you probably think about those deep-fried wings available in most sports bars, casual restaurants, and Super Bowl parties. Those are the wings made famous by Teressa Bellissimo. The Bellissimo family owned the Anchor Bar in Buffalo, New York, and their wing recipe is where buffalo wings got their start way back in 1964.

While a good deep-fried wing is hard to turn down—and I rarely turn them down if I see them at a tailgate—deep-frying doesn't leave you a lot of room for customization. That's why I grill my wings. By adding wood chunks to a charcoal grill or pellets in a smoke tube to a gas model, the smallest change gives you the chance to totally transform the taste of your wings. If you're a fan of tinkering with a recipe until you get it just right, this is a fantastic base recipe to use as a jumping-off point.

24 chicken wings, either whole or separated

2 Tbsp. baking powder

1 tsp. kosher salt

3 Tbsp. BBQ rub (page 13)

¼ cup butter

2 Tbsp. cream cheese

¾ cup Moore's Marinade Habanero Hot Sauce (or your favorite hot sauce)

3 scallions, thinly sliced

1. Remove wings from the package, rinse, and pat dry. It's very important to get the wings as dry as possible.

2. Mix together baking powder and salt in a shaker bottle and dust over the wings. You want to be sure you coat the skin lightly and evenly; this is essential to dry out the skin, which will allow for the skin to get crispy on the grill without deep-frying it.

3. Place wings in refrigerator for at least 1 to 2 hours to allow the baking powder and salt to pull the moisture out of the skin.

4. Light grill and set up for two-zone heat at 375°F.

5. Remove wings from refrigerator and lightly season with BBQ rub.

6. In medium saucepan, melt butter and cream cheese, then whisk in hot sauce. Keep warm.

7. Place wings on the grill over direct heat and turn every few minutes. You don't want them to burn, just get a nice char. When your wings get to about 150°F, move them to indirect heat and coat them with warm sauce.

8. Close lid on grill and let the sauce set up until internal temperature reaches 165°F. This will take 5–10 minutes.

9. Remove from grill, plate, garnish with scallions, and serve with your favorite dip.

GRILLED NASHVILLE HOT CHICKEN

As legend has it, this recipe was developed by a woman who wanted to teach her husband a spicy lesson about the penalties of cheating. She whipped up a batch of wings like this one to scald his lying tongue! I don't believe in using food for vengeance, but I do believe that a good hit of heat can make a dish really sing.

I've downgraded the spice level in this classic Nashville dish from "cheating spouse" to "spicy but scrumptious" so everyone can enjoy it. You'll notice most of my grilled chicken recipes feature a baking powder and salt mix—that's because this mixture is a fantastic way to dry out the chicken skin for crispy, delicious results.

If you want to serve this traditional dish like a real Nashville native, plate it with white bread and pickles. For a new twist on a Tennessee favorite, serve it with my street corn (page 138).

CHICKEN

2 Tbsp. baking powder

1 tsp. kosher salt

3 lb. chicken thighs, skin on

SEASONING

3 Tbsp. BBQ rub (page 13)

1 Tbsp. cayenne pepper

SAUCE

1 cup vegetable oil

¼ cup Moore's Marinade Habanero Hot Sauce (or your favorite hot sauce)

2 Tbsp. brown sugar

2 tsp. white pepper

1 tsp. cayenne pepper

1 tsp. garlic powder

1. Remove thighs from the package, rinse, and pat dry. The chicken needs to be as dry as possible.

2. Mix together baking powder and salt in a shaker bottle and dust over the thighs. You want to be sure you coat the skin lightly and evenly; this is essential to dry out the skin, which will allow for the skin to get crispy on the grill without deep-frying it.

3. Place chicken in refrigerator for at least 1 or 2 hours to allow the baking powder and salt to pull the moisture out of the skin.

4. Light grill and prepare for indirect heat at 375°F.

5. Remove chicken from refrigerator and season with the BBQ rub mixed with the cayenne to kick up the heat.

6. Place chicken on grill over indirect heat, close lid, and grill until internal temperature is 165°F (about 25 to 30 minutes).

7. While chicken is on grill, heat oil in medium saucepan over medium heat and whisk in all other sauce ingredients. Cook until combined (about 5 minutes). Remove from heat, but keep warm.

8. Remove chicken from grill when done, and coat in oil mixture.

9. Serve with sliced white bread and pickles.

HAWAIIAN HULI-HULI CHICKEN

The word *huli* means "turn over" in Hawaiian. It's no surprise, then, to learn that in Hawaii, this dish was traditionally cooked on a rotisserie over an open flame. I grew to love the savory and sweet taste of this chicken when I visited Hawaii as a Marine. I'd pull over at nearly every roadside chicken joint to feast on huli-huli chicken till I was ready to burst at the seams.

There's no need to buy a fancy rotisserie for this dish; I've adapted the recipe to create the traditional Hawaiian barbecue pit taste without the expense of a bunch of equipment. Make this at your next backyard barbecue and wait for your guests to marvel over the unique flavors. Serve with or without grass skirts and coconut bras.

CHICKEN

6 boneless skinless chicken breasts

2 green onions, chopped

SAUCE

1 cup brown sugar

¾ cup ketchup

½ cup low-sodium soy sauce

½ cup pineapple juice

1 Tbsp. minced fresh ginger

1 tsp. dried mustard

2 cloves garlic, minced

1. Combine all sauce ingredients in large mixing bowl and whisk together thoroughly. Set aside ½ cup of sauce in refrigerator for glazing.

2. Cut chicken filets in half crossways. Chicken breasts are not uniform in thickness from one end to the other, and cutting them this way allows the thinner pieces, which will cook faster and dry out if on the grill too long, to be removed from the grill sooner than the thicker pieces.

3. Place chicken in sealable plastic bag. Pour sauce over chicken and place in refrigerator for 8 hours or overnight.

4. Light grill and set up for two-zone heat. Take glaze out of refrigerator and allow to come up to room temperature as your grill heats up.

5. Remove chicken from plastic bag and discard sauce from plastic bag. Grill chicken breast pieces over direct heat, flipping every 2 minutes until internal temperature reaches 150°F. As the individual pieces reach the 150°F mark, move them to a plate until all pieces are off the direct heat.

6. Return chicken to the indirect heat side of grill and glaze with sauce that was set aside. Close lid and allow to cook for 5 minutes or until temperature reaches 165°F.

7. Plate, garnish with sliced green onions, and serve immediately.

HONEY BBQ-GLAZED CHICKEN DRUMSTICKS

This meal is one of my all-time favorites, and it's a staple dinner at the Grill Seeker home. It's simple and budget-friendly; you can make the whole meal for under ten bucks. What could make it even better?

These are, without question, some of the best drumsticks you'll ever eat. I said "some of" because the best drumsticks ever are still made by my mom. But she's told me several times she doesn't want to write a cookbook, so we'll have to make do with these excellent drumsticks instead.

A limited budget doesn't have to limit your flavor. Whip up these drumsticks on any night of the week and watch your family devour them.

10 to 12 chicken legs

2 Tbsp. baking powder

½ Tbsp. kosher salt

olive oil spray

2 Tbsp. BBQ rub (page 13), plus
    1 tsp. for glaze

3 Tbsp. honey

1. Remove chicken from its packaging. Rinse and pat dry with a paper towel.

2. Mix together baking powder and salt in a shaker bottle and dust over the drumsticks. You want to be sure you coat the skin lightly and evenly; this is essential to dry out the skin, which will allow for the skin to get crispy on the grill.

3. Place chicken in refrigerator for at least 1 to 2 hours to allow the baking powder and salt to pull the moisture out of the skin.

4. Light grill and set up for indirect heat at 350°F.

5. Spray drumsticks lightly with olive oil spray and generously coat with BBQ rub.

6. Place the drumsticks in a drumstick rack with drip tray if you have one. These are handy tools that can be found cheap online. If you don't have one, you can also use a foil pan, as you'll need something to catch the chicken drippings.

7. Place the rack or pan in the indirect heat and close the lid. Allow chicken to cook for about 45 minutes or until internal temperature is 165°F.

8. Remove chicken from grill and pour juices from drip pan into saucepan. Place saucepan over medium heat for 5 minutes while whisking in honey and 1 teaspoon BBQ rub.

9. Using a brush, glaze drumsticks with honey mixture.

10. Garnish and serve.

PINEAPPLE TERIYAKI TURKEY BURGERS

I'm a meat and potatoes kind of guy, and I prefer a triple bacon cheeseburger to most things in life. So when I was first asked to make a turkey burger for some guests who don't eat beef, my first thought was "ugh." Honestly, the thought of a turkey burger was about as exciting to me as a root canal. I've had turkey burgers in the past, but not often, and for good reason; they generally taste like an old shoe. I always found them to be dry and right next door to tasteless. Turkey dries out quickly because of its low fat content, though the teriyaki sauce helps prevent that.

With a heavy heart, the below is not only an edible but a *tasty* turkey burger that even a beef lover will enjoy. If you're feeling a bit ambitious, try also adding some blistered shishito peppers (page 131); they go well with sweet pineapple and make for a grand presentation.

1 tsp. BBQ rub (page 13)

1 can sliced pineapple

4 slices Swiss cheese

1 cup fresh raw spinach, stems removed

4 sets of hamburger buns

PATTY

1 lb. ground turkey

½ cup bread crumbs

¼ cup teriyaki sauce

1 small yellow onion, diced

2 Tbsp. finely chopped parsley

2 cloves garlic, minced

1 egg, beaten

1. In a large mixing bowl, combine all patty ingredients and mix thoroughly by hand.
2. Divide mixture into four equal parts. Form the four portions into patties and lay on parchment paper.
3. Sprinkle each patty evenly with BBQ rub.
4. Place in refrigerator for 30 minutes while you light your grill.
5. Light grill and set up for medium-high direct heat.
6. Place burgers and pineapple slices over direct heat. Grill the pineapple till it gets a nice char on both sides. Grill burgers till they are done, about 4 minutes on each side, with a 90-degree turn at each two-minute mark. After burgers are flipped over, add a slice of Swiss cheese to each patty and allow to melt as patty finishes cooking.
7. Remove from grill. Layer burgers on buns with spinach and pineapple.

SWEET THAI CILANTRO CHILI CHICKEN QUARTERS

BBQ chicken is one of the great pleasures in life, and there are many ways to do it. I was introduced to this Thai take on the classic while on one of my many stopovers on Wake Island. As a young Marine in the middle of the Pacific Ocean, halfway between Hawaii and Japan, I was convinced that those mess hall workers could make an old boot taste like a gourmet steak. The trick was the unique flavors they used to spruce up simple ingredients.

This recipe has a bit of a kick to it, but it's balanced by a perfect hit of sweetness. Serve this over a bed of white rice or pan-seared ramen noodles. If you like the taste of this dish, consider whipping up the sauce to use on a light fish, like mahi-mahi.

4 chicken leg quarters, lightly coated with olive oil

1 cup and 1 tsp. water

¾ cup rice vinegar

½ cup white sugar

3 Tbsp. freshly chopped cilantro

2 Tbsp. freshly minced ginger root

2 tsp. freshly minced garlic

2 Tbsp. crushed red pepper flakes

2 Tbsp. ketchup

2 Tbsp. cornstarch

2 Tbsp. fresh basil chiffonade ("chiffonade" is fancy for "thinly sliced")

1. Light grill and set up for two-zone heat at 350°F.

2. In a medium-sized saucepan, bring 1 cup water and the vinegar to a boil over high heat.

3. Stir in sugar, cilantro, ginger, garlic, red pepper flakes, and ketchup; simmer for 5 minutes.

4. In small mixing bowl, mix together 1 teaspoon warm water and 2 tablespoons cornstarch. Use a fork for mixing this, and what you'll end up with will resemble white school glue.

5. Slowly whisk the cornstarch mixture into the simmering sauce, and continue mixing until sauce thickens. Set aside.

6. Place oiled chicken quarters over direct heat, skin side down, for 3 minutes or until grill marks form. Flip chicken to bone side and grill for an additional 5 minutes.

7. Move chicken to indirect heat, close lid on grill, and let cook until internal temperature reaches 155°F.

8. At 155°F internal temperature, glaze chicken with sauce and allow to finish cooking to an internal temperature of 165°F.

9. Plate, garnish with basil, and serve.

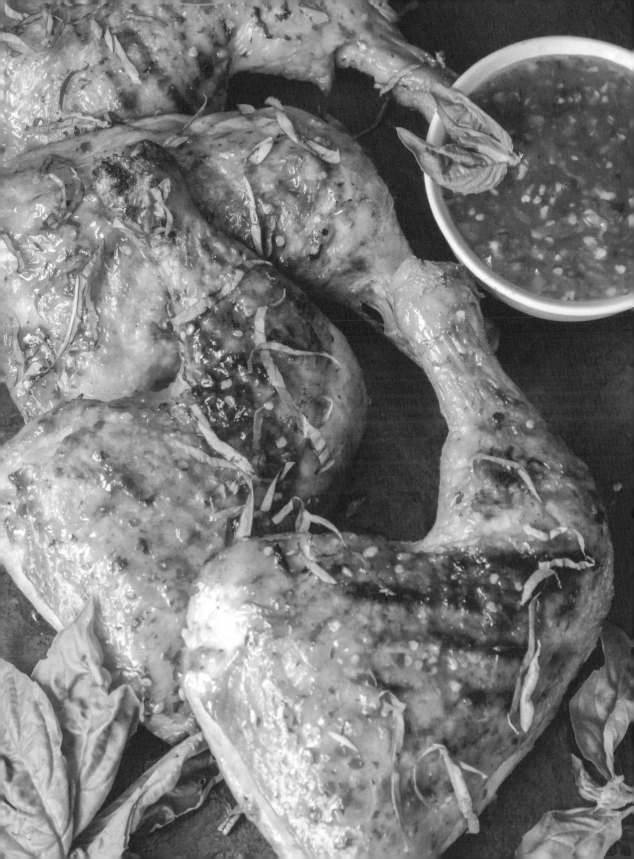

• CHAPTER SIX •

PORK, VEAL, AND LAMB

APRICOT-GLAZED DOUBLE-CUT PORK CHOPS

Pork chops are a staple dinner in my house. They're hearty, delicious, and fairly simple to prepare. It is true that pork is easy to overcook, but I've simplified the process for you with this easy recipe for two-zone cooking.

The secret here is to cook the chop on the bone. A lot has been said about improving flavor via bone-in cooking before, but this much is scientific fact: bones are natural heat conductors, and though they cause meat to cook more slowly, they also help regulate the temperature. This means that if you tend to overcook your food, bone-in grilling is the way to go.

One bite of these bone-in chops with the sweet and savory apricot glaze and you'll understand why it's a family favorite at my house.

PORK CHOPS

2 double-cut bone-in pork chops

2 tsp. smoked salt (page 22)

SAUCE

1 cup apricot preserves

¼ cup reduced-sodium chicken broth

¼ cup soy sauce

1 Tbsp. Dijon mustard

1 tsp. garlic powder

1 tsp. ground ginger

1. Light grill and prepare for two-zone heat at 285°F.

2. In a small saucepan over medium heat, combine all sauce ingredients and whisk together.

3. Lightly dust pork chops with your favorite smoked salt, and place in indirect side of grill. Cook until pork reaches an internal temperature of 130°F (about 30-40 minutes).

4. At internal temperature of 130°F, place pork over direct heat, searing all sides (about 3 minutes each side).

5. Place pork back on indirect heat, glaze with sauce, and close lid. Allow sauce to set for 5 minutes as pork finishes. The USDA recommends 145°F for pork chops. I personally usually go a little less, but I have to recommend following USDA guidelines.

6. Remove from grill, plate, and serve with remaining sauce.

CAVEMAN-STYLE VEAL CHOPS

Sometimes it's good to get back to your roots . . . *way* back. You don't have to wear furs while you grill this delicious chop dinner or hunt the veal using a spear—but if that's your thing, go for it. This caveman dish is exciting to cook and produces a sear that you can only get by going primal. Gather the family around for the cooking process. It's fun to watch and might get your kids interested in cooking!

The key is to get good lump charcoal for the cook, and be prepared to flip. If you use high-quality charcoal, you shouldn't have the problem of getting ash on the meat. Just be sure to flip the chop frequently because the sear will be intense and quick. It's also a good idea to invest in some heavy-duty metal tongs because nothing ruins a good veal chop faster than melted rubber.

2 bone-in veal chops
(about 1 inch thick)

MARINADE

1 small shallot, finely chopped

2 cloves garlic, minced

3 Tbsp. chopped fresh rosemary

1 Tbsp. tarragon

½ cup olive oil

juice from ½ lemon

½ tsp. rosemary salt (page 19)

½ tsp. fresh cracked black pepper

1. Mix all marinade ingredients thoroughly in a mixing bowl.
2. Place veal chops in a sealable plastic bag and pour marinade over them. Seal bag and massage marinade so it completely coats the veal. Place in refrigerator and allow to marinate 4–6 hours or overnight.
3. Light grill using lump charcoal, with cooking grates removed. Ensure an even distribution of coals, not a mound of coals forming a peak. Allow coals to reach a white-hot ashed-over appearance.
4. Remove veal from bag and blot off any excess marinade with a paper towel.
5. Prepare coals by blowing off any loose ash that has formed.
6. Using a sturdy set of tongs, place veal directly on coals. The sear you get from this is pretty intense, so be prepared to flip often, about every 60 seconds. Ensure that when you flip the veal, you place it in various places on the coal bed. The coals will begin to cool immediately when the meat is placed on them, so using new "hot spots" on the coal is key.
7. Cook veal to an internal temperature of 140°F. This should take a total of about 10 minutes depending the thickness of the chops.
8. Remove from heat and let rest for 5 minutes, during which time carryover cooking will bring the veal up to 145°F.
9. Plate and serve with roasted carrots or your favorite fresh seasonal vegetable.

PORK, VEAL, AND LAMB

CINNAMON-BRINED GRILLED PORK CHOPS

Thinly cut pork chops can dry out quickly. It's one of the reasons many of us grow up thinking pork is too dry. (Not that I ever did . . . Don't read this part, Mom.) But these thin chops can be a juicy and inexpensive dinner if you know how to cook them properly. You'll be able to save money and still serve a dish that tastes like a million bucks.

Brining the chops adds moisture and ensures that the meat you serve will have people drooling instead of reaching for their water. The best part? The brine trick works on more than pork. Use it on everything from red meat to poultry for moist, delicious meals.

There's also a hidden benefit to this recipe: Preparing this brine makes your house smell amazing. Think of the money you'll save on potpourri!

apple cinnamon brine
   (page 12)

8 thin-cut bone-in pork chops
   (½- to ¾-inch cuts)

TIP:
THESE CHOPS PAIR EXCELLENTLY WITH THE SMOKED APPLE CRUMBLE ON PAGE 164.

1. Prepare brine as described on page 12, and let cool to room temperature.

2. While brine cools, use a Jaccard meat tenderizer to pierce the entire surface of both sides of the pork chops. If you don't have a Jaccard, don't run out and buy one for this. You can use a fork and just do a thorough job of piercing the meat so that the brine can penetrate. It will take a bit longer, but a fork will get the job done.

3. Pour room-temperature brine into large container, add pork chops so they are completely covered, and place in refrigerator for 24 hours.

4. After pork has brined, light grill and set up for high direct heat.

5. Remove chops from brine and dab dry with a paper towel. This step is important because we are searing these chops hot and fast over direct heat. Any surface moisture will impede the searing process; the meat won't actually sear until the brine evaporates, causing the pork to steam in the process—not good!

6. Place chops over screaming hot coals with grill grate as close to coals as possible. If using a gas grill, preheat for as long as needed in order to get grate as hot as possible.

7. After grilling for 90 seconds, turn chops 90 degrees and sear for an additional 90 seconds. Flip chops and repeat.

8. Depending on the thickness of the chops, they should be done at this point, but remember to always use a dependable meat thermometer to check internal temperature of the pork chops for doneness. I recommend taking them off the grill at 140°F, as the carryover cooking (while the chops are resting) will put them at a safe eating temperature as recommended by the USDA.

9. Let chops rest 5 minutes, plate, and serve.

GRILLED SPAGHETTI AND MEATBALLS

Let's be real: anyone can boil noodles. We all know what they taste like, and while they're fine, they're not exactly exciting.

Want to really impress your friends at the next dinner party? Invite them into the backyard, then nonchalantly throw some spaghetti into a grill pan and wait for the questions to start. Why grill spaghetti, other than as a cool conversation starter? Because the intense heat of the grill and the flavor of the charcoal add texture, char, and excitement to an otherwise boring dish.

So invite over some witnesses, grill up some spaghetti, and impress your dinner guests with an unexpected and tasty twist on an Italian classic.

MEATBALLS

1 lb. ground beef

½ lb. ground pork

½ lb. ground veal

3 cloves garlic, minced

2 eggs, beaten

1½ cups Italian bread crumbs

½ cup fresh grated Parmesan cheese

½ medium Vidalia onion, finely chopped

3 Tbsp. chopped flat-leaf parsley + 1 Tbsp. for garnish

1 tsp. kosher salt

1 tsp. black pepper

¾ cup warm water

SPAGHETTI

1 lb. dried spaghetti noodles

2 Tbsp. olive oil

1 Tbsp. kosher salt

1. Light grill and prepare for two-zone heat at 325°F.

2. In large mixing bowl, add all meatball ingredients except the water and roughly mix. Gradually add in warm water and continue to mix till well incorporated.

3. Form mixture into 2-inch balls, making sure not to pack them too tight. This will make about 16 to 20 meatballs. Place them on a cooling rack.

4. Add a chunk of pecan (or your favorite smoking wood) to hot coals; if using a gas grill, use a smoker tube with pellets. Place cooling rack with meatballs on indirect heat. Cook for 20 minutes or until done based on internal temperature.

5. While meatballs are cooking, bring large pot of salted water to a boil and boil spaghetti noodles for half the recommended time according to the package.

6. Drain water from noodles. Add olive oil and toss to coat the noodles.

7. Using a grill basket over direct heat, add spaghetti noodles and toss constantly till done (about 5 minutes).

8. Plate noodles and top with meatballs and your favorite sauce. Garnish with flat-leaf parsley.

GRILLED STUFFED PORK TENDERLOIN

Pork tenderloin is one of those dishes that seem intimidating. It can dry out easily and looks complex when you see it served. But I have a secret pork tenderloin recipe that is an easy way to create a dish that looks like a Pinterest post and tastes like a gourmet meal.

There are two keys to this dish: the roll cut and the cheese. It may take some practice to perfect your roll cut—which just means spiral cutting the tenderloin so it can be rolled into that trademark pinwheel shape—but it's worth the knife work. Do a quick internet search and you'll find tons of videos on it, but simply put, imagine laying a roll of paper towels on a table and rolling the roll in order to unroll it. That's what you're doing with a roll cut.

Until you've got that skill down, however, my advice is to add more cheese. I'm on record as believing that everything is better with extra cheese, and this loin is no exception. If your roll cut is a little uneven, add some extra cheese to fill in any gaps. If your roll cut is perfect, just add the extra cheese because cheese is delicious.

This recipe will have the family asking for seconds and maybe even pulling out their phones to post your dinner on Instagram. Don't forget to tag me!

1½ Tbsp. olive oil, plus a drizzle

½ medium Vidalia onion, finely chopped

1 tsp. Worcestershire sauce

6 oz. chopped baby bella mushrooms

2 cloves garlic, minced

2 tsp. minced rosemary

4 fresh sage leaves, chopped

½ tsp. celery salt

½ tsp. fresh black pepper

¼ cup chopped flat-leaf parsley

2 cups fresh spinach leaves, stems removed

2 tsp. Dijon mustard

1 pork tenderloin, 1½ to 2 lb.

4 slices pancetta

4 slices provolone cheese

2 tsp. rosemary salt (page 19)

1. In a medium skillet, heat olive oil over medium heat. Add onion and cook for 1 minute before adding Worcestershire sauce, mushrooms, garlic, rosemary, sage, celery salt, and black pepper. Constantly mixing with wooden spoon, cook down till mushrooms are soft (5–7 minutes).

2. Add parsley and spinach. Continue to mix with wooden spoon. Cook until spinach starts to wilt. Stir in mustard and cook for additional 1 minute. Remove from heat, set aside, and allow to cool while you prep the pork.

3. Light grill and set up for two-zone heat.

4. Place pork tenderloin on cutting board, and with your knife parallel to the cutting surface, roll cut the tenderloin so it's about ½-inch thick when unrolled.

5. Once pork has been roll cut, lay pancetta on top, followed by provolone cheese and spinach mixture. Leave about a 1-inch border around the edge of the loin.

6. Roll tenderloin back up and truss together with butcher's twine. (If you're not sure how to truss, just tie the roll up using a simple square knot every 2 inches, but trussing is super easy. If I can do it, anyone can; you don't need to be a sailor or an Eagle Scout. An Internet search will bring up ample videos about how to do it.)

7. Drizzle outside of roll with a very thin coat of olive oil and sprinkle with rosemary salt.

8. Place pork over high direct heat, turn often, and sear outside of roll till golden brown.

9. Move to indirect heat, establish temperature at 350°F, and continue to cook with lid closed for about 30 minutes or until internal temperature is 145°F.

10. Remove from grill, slice, and serve.

LAMB LOIN CHOPS WITH BASIL OIL

Lamb is a far more versatile meat than it gets credit for. There's more to lamb than kebabs and gyros, people! These loin chops are a great way to experience a versatile cut of meat; think of them as tiny porterhouse steaks. The loin is packed with flavor and is melt-in-your-mouth tender, especially if you serve it medium rare. Be mindful of the timing, though, because they cook quickly.

Prepare the basil oil ahead of time—in fact, it tastes best if you allow it to sit at least overnight before serving. If you're a fan of garlic, throw a few roasted cloves into the oil to give it a little kick. While a perfect complement to the lamb, this oil is a versatile treat. Put it on chicken or pizza, dunk some grilled French bread in it, or even eat it by the spoonful. (What happens in the kitchen stays in the kitchen.)

The key to perfecting this oil is blanching the basil first, so your oil doesn't turn an unappetizing brown color after a few days. If you blanch your basil, you'll have a gorgeous oil that will last for weeks. I'm not kidding about it being pretty. A jar of this oil sits on my table at all times; it's one of my favorite, and most delicious, centerpieces.

LAMB

8 lamb loin chops

1 Tbsp. olive oil

1 tsp. salt

OIL

2 packed cups basil, washed with stems removed

¾ cup olive oil

1 tsp. sea salt

1. Light grill and set up for high direct heat.
2. In a medium saucepan, bring 3 cups water to rolling boil.
3. Prepare a medium mixing bowl three-fourths full of water and ice.
4. Drop basil into boiling water for 15 seconds, remove, and immediate place into ice water bath to stop the cooking process. Stir the basil around to ensure it has cooled sufficiently and stopped cooking.
5. Remove from ice bath and place on paper towel, cover with additional paper towel, and press gently to dry the basil.
6. In a small bullet-style mixer or food processor, add basil, olive oil, and sea salt. Blend till basil is fully incorporated. Mix will become a brilliant green color. Place in glass jar and set aside.
7. Lightly coat lamb chops with olive oil and season with salt.
8. Place on grill directly over high heat for 3 minutes.
9. Flip chops and grill additional 3 minutes until done.
10. Plate, drizzle chops with basil oil, and serve.

ROSEMARY LAMB RIB CHOPS WITH GRILLED RAMPS

Let's be honest: there's something pretty cool about serving bone-in chops. The bones in this recipe are frenched, which makes them sound fancy, but I prefer to think of them as "meat handles." Grab on and dig in; this recipe is too good to worry about table manners.

Rib chops are similar to loin chops in tenderness, but their higher fat content means more flavor. The lamb here is powerful but subtle. Don't do too much to this cut of meat or you could lose the unique taste. In fact, the only thing I recommend doing to rib chops is rubbing them down with some of my rosemary salt, which makes this preparation one of the simplest in the book. If you want to get extra fancy and add a bright note to the dish, forgo the salt and serve these chops with my chimichurri sauce (page 56).

If you're a fan of rare meat, slice the chops individually from the rack and serve them straight from the grill. If you like them a little more done, slice them from the rack, and sear both sides briefly on the grill—the added char flavor is hard to beat. Ramps are a great complement to these chops, like scallions fused with garlic. In spite of their short harvest season, they are one of my favorite ingredients to search for at the farmers market.

Simple to make but fancy to behold, these chops are an impressive dish that looks great at a tailgate or as the centerpiece on a holiday table.

2 racks lamb chops

24 ramps, washed with root end trimmed

2 Tbsp. olive oil, divided

1 Tbsp. rosemary salt (page 19)

1 tsp. sea salt

1 tsp. fresh squeezed lemon juice

1. Light grill and set up for two-zone heat at 350°F.
2. Rub racks of lamb with 1 tablespoon of olive oil and dust with rosemary salt.
3. Place lamb on grill over indirect heat, close lid, and grill till internal temperature reaches 105°F.
4. Remove lamb and allow direct heat portion of the grill to intensify.
5. Toss ramps with remaining tablespoon of olive oil.
6. Slice lamb racks into single chops and place over direct heat. Grill 1 to 2 minutes on each side.
7. Place ramps over direct heat and grill till a nice char is formed, turning occasionally (about 3 minutes total).
8. Remove lamb chops and ramps and plate. Season ramps with sea salt and a drizzle of lemon juice.

SMOKED EGGS AND CHORIZO SAUSAGE

Breakfast is by far and away my favorite meal of the day. I'm here to tell you, breakfast isn't just for mornings, at least not at my house. Aside from being delicious, it's a fun change of pace to have a "breakfast for dinner" day. Add to that cooking breakfast on the grill, and it increases the fun factor times ten on this meal. This skillet incorporates many of my favorite things, and the quick cook time means your eggs will be kissed with just the tiniest hint of smoke. I prefer the runny yolks of this recipe, but if that's not your thing, you can roughly beat the eggs and cream together before putting them in the pan.

For those that like the heat, I highly suggest using a dab of your favorite hot sauce on this one too!

1 tsp. olive oil

5 to 6 large eggs

¼ cup heavy cream

½ lb. chorizo sausage, crumbled

½ lb. kielbasa, sliced

½ tsp. kosher salt

½ cup shredded cheddar cheese

2 Tbsp. chopped chives

1. Light grill and set up for indirect heat at 325°F.
2. In a 12-inch cast-iron pan, evenly spread olive oil on bottom and sides to prevent eggs from sticking.
3. Crack eggs into pan.
4. Pour heavy cream all over the egg whites.
5. Sprinkle crumbled chorizo on egg whites.
6. Place sliced kielbasa in gaps between egg yolks.
7. Sprinkle salt over entire skillet.
8. Evenly spread cheese over egg whites.
9. Add one wood chunk of your choice to hot coals; if using a gas grill, use a smoke tube with pellets. Place skillet over indirect heat.
10. Close lid and let cook 13–15 minutes till egg whites are firm and yolks are still a bit runny.
11. Remove from grill, top with chives, and serve hot.

SPICY ITALIAN SAUSAGE, MUSHROOM, AND BASIL PIZZA

If I had to choose between pizza or tacos, I honestly don't know what I'd do. Having to pick only one may be the very definition of cruel and unusual punishment. I am a huge fan of both, but what may give pizza the edge is the fun of making it from scratch with the family on a Friday night.

Pizza dough gets a bad rap for being difficult to make, but it really isn't. Recruit the family to help in the process and it can actually be not only easy but infinitely more fun than that grueling game of Monopoly that never really gets finished, or the never-ending argument about what movie to choose for the evening's fun.

I happen to love these toppings, but this is one of those recipes that allow for a ton of latitude relative to the toppings used. The sky is really the limit. For example, try replacing the pizza sauce with BBQ sauce and using some leftover chicken instead of sausage. This crust, which is the real star of the show here, can also be used for the flatbreads on page 30.

PIZZA DOUGH

4 cups bread flour

2 Tbsp. granulated garlic

2 tsp. sugar

1 envelope instant yeast

3 tsp. kosher salt

1 tsp. black pepper

1½ cups hot water, about 110°F, to activate the yeast

3 Tbsp. olive oil

PIZZA TOPPINGS

1½ cups pizza sauce

3 cups shredded mozzarella cheese

2 cups spicy Italian sausage

2 cups sliced mushrooms

1 Tbsp. olive oil

¾ cup chopped basil leaves

PIZZA DOUGH

1. Combine the flour, garlic, sugar, yeast, salt, and pepper in the bowl of a stand mixer with a bread hook. Turn the mixer on low and add the hot water and olive oil. Mix until the dough is in the shape of a ball. If the dough is sticking to the bowl or your fingers, you may have to add some additional flour, but don't add too much at one time or your dough will get too dry. If that happens, just add a little more water till it gets to the desired consistency.

2. Place the dough onto a lightly floured hard surface, such as a countertop, and knead until the dough is formed into a nice tight ball shape.

3. Place ball of dough into lightly greased bowl and coat the dough with a thin coat of olive oil. Cover with plastic wrap and let sit at room temperature for 1 hour. At that time, the dough should have doubled in size.

4. Once the dough has doubled in size, cut the dough into 2 equal pieces, reshape each piece into a ball, and let them rest on a floured surface under the plastic wrap for about 10 minutes. After the rest, shape the balls of dough into 12- or 13-inch circles.

5. Note: While dough is rising, preheat grill to 575°F. Place pizza stone on grill so the stone is preheated when you place the pizza on it.

PIZZA

1. Once the dough is rolled out, add ¾ cup of pizza sauce to each pizza and spread evenly, leaving about an inch border at the edge.

2. Sprinkle 1½ cups of mozzarella cheese, 1 cup Italian sausage, and 1 cup mushrooms all over each pizza.

3. Brush the edge of the pizza crust with olive oil. This will help the crust get that crisp golden-brown color we all love.

4. Place the pizza onto the hot pizza stone for 7 minutes. Remove from the grill and top with basil.

5. Allow to cool for a few minutes, cut, and serve.

TOMAHAWK PORK CHOP WITH SWEET ONION AND BACON BBQ SAUCE

This meal is a showstopper. Set it down in front of a hungry crowd and watch as they all struggle between picking up their forks and picking up their phones to broadcast their dinner to social media. It's hard to blame them. With a dramatic bone-in presentation and gorgeous char, this is truly a picture-perfect presentation.

Tomahawk chops don't just look impressive; they are a flavorful cut that cooks beautifully. The fat on the chop keeps the pork moist during cooking, and in case that isn't enough to convince you, I'll mention that there's bacon in the glaze. Raw onion mixed with BBQ bacon sauce guarantees great taste with every bite. This is a hearty chop that will tempt you to grab it by the bone and go caveman. But don't worry, your guests will join you.

SAUCE

1 Tbsp. olive oil

2 slices bacon, roughly chopped

2 cloves garlic, minced

½ medium sweet onion, diced

1 cup ketchup

¼ cup molasses

½ cup brown sugar

¼ cup honey

2 Tbsp. apple cider vinegar

1 Tbsp. Worcestershire sauce

1 tsp. salt

CHOPS

2 large tomahawk pork chops, about 1.5 in. thick

1 Tbsp. BBQ rub (page 13)

1. Light grill and set up for two-zone heat at 275°–300°F.

2. Heat the oil in a medium saucepan over high heat. Add bacon pieces and cook till crispy. Remove bacon and save for a salad topper or breakfast burrito (whatever you like).

3. Reduce heat to medium and add garlic and onion to rendered bacon fat. Cook for 5 minutes, until onions become translucent. Be careful not to burn the garlic.

4. Reduce the heat to low and add ketchup, molasses, brown sugar, honey, vinegar, Worcestershire sauce, and salt. Mix well.

5. Using an immersion blender, blend all chunks of onion into the sauce and allow to simmer over low heat for 20 minutes.

6. While sauce is simmering, lightly dust chops with BBQ rub and place them on indirect side of grill, close lid, and cook for 20 minutes.

7. Open lid after 20 minutes and move chops over intense direct heat, searing both sides for 90 seconds each.

8. Return to indirect heat, glaze with sauce, and close lid, cooking for an additional 5 minutes or until internal pork temperature is 145°F. The sauce will "set" during this step and will become a beautiful dark mahogany color.

9. Plate and garnish with raw onion rings as desired.

· CHAPTER SEVEN ·

SEAFOOD

GRILLED HONEY, GARLIC, AND GINGER SHRIMP

Cooking after a long day of work can be a daunting task. You're tired, you're hungry, and the takeout menu is *right there*. Ordering out is an understandable impulse, but you don't have to give in if you have this recipe on hand.

Garlic and ginger are a classic combination, and this recipe brings them together for a flavorful, fast meal that will immediately brighten up your weeknights. The best part? It's a healthy dinner that doesn't compromise on taste. Even if you're exhausted, you can spoil yourself with delicious food that doesn't require a lot of effort.

Fire up the grill, toss in the shrimp, and you're done in the same amount of time it would take for the takeout place to find your house. It's so good you might even leave yourself a tip.

2 lb. extra-large shrimp, peeled and deveined

½ cup olive oil

2 cloves fresh garlic, minced

½ medium shallot, minced

¼ cup honey

4 tsp. ground ginger

1 tsp. dried dill

1. Heat olive oil over medium heat and add shallot and garlic. Cook for 3–5 minutes until shallot becomes translucent.

2. Add in remaining ingredients, minus the shrimp, and heat for 2–3 minutes. Remove sauce from heat, divide in half, and let cool to room temperature.

3. Light grill and set up for high direct heat.

4. Toss shrimp with half of sauce, coating thoroughly, and place on nonstick grill pan. The grill pan isn't a requirement; you can also use skewers, but you'll need one or the other, because shrimp tend to fall through the grates of a standard grill.

5. Place grill grate directly over heat on grill. Allow shrimp to cook for 3 minutes, leaving lid open.

6. Turn shrimp and baste with remaining sauce, close lid, and allow to cook for 5 minutes.

7. Remove from grill and serve hot.

TIP:
YOU'LL KNOW THE SHRIMP ARE DONE WHEN THEY START TO TURN WHITE AND CURL UP SLIGHTLY. SHRIMP OVERCOOK QUICKLY, SO MONITOR CLOSELY.

GRILLED PRAWNS WITH ROASTED GARLIC AND DILL BUTTER

After a long day at work and a tedious commute, you finally get home, and the last thing you want to do is cook. We've all been there. Before you reach for a takeout menu or consider eating just chips for dinner, open to this recipe.

These prawns grill in a flash, are healthier than whatever combo you were going to order at the drive-thru, and taste great. The key to this meal is the butter, which you can make ahead of time and keep in the refrigerator. Just butterfly the prawns, fire up the grill, and you're minutes away from a nutritious, delicious meal.

This recipe is also a lifesaver if you forgot about a dinner party. Cook up a batch of these butter-basted prawns and bring them to a friend's house for an eye-catching appetizer that will earn you raves. It only *looks* like you spent all day preparing them!

6 to 8 giant prawns

2 Tbsp. olive oil

1 tsp. sea salt

2 lemons, cut in half

roasted garlic and dill butter
  (page 18)

1. Light grill and set up for medium-high direct heat.

2. Using a sharp knife, slice prawns in half lengthwise from head to tail. Pull meat from shell, leaving the tail attached, and remove vein.

3. Rinse the prawn halves under cold water to remove the organs and internals from the head area. (Some people will eat this, but not this guy.)

4. Tuck meat back into shell and drizzle prawn halves with olive oil and sea salt.

5. Place lemon halves, cut side down, over direct heat, and grill till evenly charred.

6. Place prawns over direct heat, meat side down, and grill for 2 to 3 minutes, depending on the size of the prawns.

7. Flip prawns to meat side up and top with garlic and dill butter. Close lid on grill and cook an additional 3 minutes, allowing the butter to melt on and around the meat inside the shell.

8. Remove from grill and serve with charred lemon.

TIP:
SAVE THE SHELLS FROM YOUR PRAWNS AND USE THEM TO MAKE A SEAFOOD STOCK.

GRILLED TERIYAKI-GLAZED COHO SALMON

Salmon is one of my favorite proteins. But it can be a rather divisive fish—with its bold flavor and meaty texture, people either love it or hate it. I would argue that most people who hate salmon don't know how diverse it is, or perhaps they've been eating "farm-raised" salmon instead of wild-caught. Check out the blog entry on my website for the real story of farm-raised salmon. Plus, many don't know that the taste of salmon can mellow or brighten depending on the glazes and sauces you pair with it.

If you think salmon isn't for you, it might be because you haven't had it with the right pairing yet. Because the fish is so versatile, there's plenty of room to experiment. Blackened, raw, smoked, baked, grilled, or fried, salmon is a fish that can do it all. It also takes on the flavors of marinades beautifully, infusing the fish with whatever tastes you prefer. Try this classic teriyaki glaze with a touch of smoke and discover just how hearty and flavorful this fish can be.

1-2 coho salmon filets

SAUCE

1 cup water

¼ cup brown sugar

¼ cup soy sauce

1 Tbsp. honey

1½ Tbsp. finely minced ginger root (about 1-inch piece)

2 cloves garlic, finely minced

½ tsp. white pepper

THICKENER

2 Tbsp. cornstarch

¼ cup cold water

1. Light grill and set up for indirect heat at 325°F.

2. In medium saucepan over medium heat, combine sauce ingredients and bring to a low boil.

3. Once sauce reaches a low boil, use a fork and mix together cornstarch and water in separate bowl until thoroughly incorporated. Slowly whisk cornstarch mixture into sauce until it thickens.

4. Add one chunk of pecan wood to the hot coals of your grill; if you're using a gas grill, use a smoke tube with pecan pellets.

5. Brush sauce onto salmon filets, place over indirect heat, close lid, and cook for 15 minutes.

6. Brush salmon with another coat of sauce, close lid, and cook for an additional 10 minutes.

7. Remove from grill, garnish, and serve hot.

LEMON- AND HERB-STUFFED RED SNAPPER WITH CILANTRO-BASIL DRIZZLE

Red snapper, while an odd-looking fish with a fairly big head, scary-looking teeth, and brilliant red hue, is a favorite among grillers because of its light, almost sweet taste that makes it so incredibly versatile. You can take this in so many directions; the sky really is the limit for this lean yet extremely moist fish. The bones pull out fairly easily, but be cautious when digging in because you're bound to miss a few here or there (and let me tell you, biting into one isn't fun). When you pick this fish up from your local butcher or fishmonger, be sure you ask them to scale the fish (that job gets messy on your own), and depending on the source, they may even stuff and tie it for you. It never hurts to ask.

STUFFING

1 whole red snapper (about 5 lb., scales removed)

¼ cup fresh basil

½ large lemon, sliced (save other half for cilantro-basil drizzle)

drizzle of olive oil

dusting of sea salt

CILANTRO-BASIL SAUCE

¾ cup olive oil

¾ cup fresh basil

¼ cup cilantro

1 tsp. sea salt, divided in half

½ large lemon, for zest and juice

drizzle of olive oil

2 whole lemons

3 sprigs oregano

1. Stuff cavity of fish with basil, oregano, lemon slices, drizzle of olive oil, and light dusting of sea salt.

2. Using butcher's twine, tie up your fish so the stuffing stays in place. Place fish in sealable bag and put in refrigerator for the day, or overnight if possible. This allows the flavors of the lemon and herbs to infuse the fish from inside.

3. Light grill and prepare for medium direct heat. For a gas grill, this is done with the turn of a knob; for a charcoal grill, just use fewer coals (a pile about the size of two fists) and set grilling grate 7–10 inches above coals.

4. To make cilantro-basil sauce, in a small blender or food processor, combine olive oil, basil, cilantro, ½ teaspoon sea salt, and lemon zest and juice. Blend till fully incorporated into a smooth liquid. Place in refrigerator till needed.

5. Remove fish from refrigerator, drizzle a light coat of olive oil on both sides, and sprinkle with remaining ½ teaspoon of sea salt. Place in fish basket if you have one. (Trust me, it makes flipping the fish so much easier, and red snapper can be a challenge to flip without one.)

6. Cut two lemons in half and remove any visible seeds.

7. Place fish and lemon halves, cut side down, over direct heat.

8. Remove lemons from grill once they start to brown up and caramelize (about 4 minutes).

9. Turn fish as skin starts to flake. This will vary with size of fish, but watch for this to happen anywhere between 6 and 10 minutes. Flip fish and cook for an additional 6 to 10 minutes, till the flesh starts to flake and brown.

10. Remove from grill and serve with cilantro-basil sauce and caramelized lemon halves.

SEARED SEA SCALLOPS WITH ROASTED GARLIC AND DILL BUTTER

With scallops, timing is everything. Overcook them, and you've essentially made very expensive rubber balls. The key is to be sure the scallops are very dry when you sear them; if they're not dry, the moisture will steam and overcook the scallops before you get your sear. Once you get a feel for scallops, however, you'll be amazed how quickly and beautifully they color. Pair them with my premade garlic and dill butter for a lavish feast.

This recipe utilizes one of my favorite kitchen tools—the cast-iron pan. There's not much you can't accomplish with a well-seasoned cast-iron pan. (You could even forgo the grill and sear these scallops on a stovetop.)

So why fire up the grill? Because these scallops pair perfectly with grilled cilantro lime sweet potatoes (page 132) or grilled rosemary Parmesan potatoes (page 136). Just divide the grill in half, set the cast-iron pan on the rack, and cook your sides at the same time! It's the Grill Seeker version of a one-pot dinner!

12-18 medium-sized scallops

1 tsp. kosher salt

1 lemon

2 Tbsp. roasted garlic and dill butter (page 18)

2 tsp. olive oil

1. Light grill and set up for high direct heat.
2. Rinse scallops in cold water and dry thoroughly with a paper towel.
3. Season scallops lightly with kosher salt.
4. Slice lemon into ¼-inch thick slices and remove seeds.
5. Place cast-iron pan directly over hot coals. Melt butter and olive oil in pan.
6. Gently place the scallops and lemon slices into the oil and butter. Be careful not to let the scallops touch each other in the pan.
7. Sear for 90 seconds on each side. A nice crust will form on both sides of the scallop, with the middle remaining relatively opaque.
8. Serve hot.

TIP:
THE ACIDITY OF THE CITRUS WILL TEND TO DISCOLOR A LESS THAN HIGHLY SEASONED CAST-IRON PAN. FOR THIS REASON, I RECOMMEND USING A WELL-SEASONED PAN FOR THIS RECIPE WITH APPROPRIATE CAST-IRON MAINTENANCE RIGHT AFTER USE. ALTERNATIVELY, YOU CAN USE A STAINLESS-STEEL PAN IF YOUR CAST-IRON GAME ISN'T ON POINT.

SKEWERED SHRIMPS ON FIRE WITH CHARRED LEMON

How do you turn something sour into something sweet? Add a little heat. At least, that's the key for lemons. We all know that a raw lemon is sour when you bite into it. When you char lemons on the grill, however, the fruit takes on a sweet flavor that pairs beautifully with shrimp.

We're also going to go over the basics of grilling with skewers in this recipe, since trying to flip two pounds of shrimp on the grill individually would probably result in half your shrimp being burned and half undercooked. Skewers make cooking small items evenly on the grill a breeze, and they look great when you're plating. If you want an Instagram-worthy grill, try using a skewer—and remember to tag me!

2 cloves garlic, minced

¼ cup olive oil

1 Tbsp. Moore's Marinade Habanero Hot Sauce, or your favorite hot sauce

2 tsp. smoked salt (page 22) or coarse sea salt

1 tsp. Hungarian hot paprika

juice from ½ fresh lemon

2 lb. large raw shrimp, peeled and deveined

2 lemons, cut in half seeds removed

1. Combine all ingredients into a medium-size mixing bowl and whisk together. Mixture will be rather thick.

2. Pour mixture into a sealable bag and add in shrimp. Seal bag and massage shrimp to fully cover with mixture.

3. Place in refrigerator for at least 2 hours.

4. After shrimp has marinated, light grill and prepare for high direct heat.

5. Remove shrimp from bag and place on skewers, brushing any leftover marinade onto the shrimp.

6. Place shrimp skewers and lemon halves, cut side down, directly over hot coals. Lemons should go on cut side down in order to char them and create a sweet lemon freshness.

7. After 2 minutes turn shrimp and rotate lemon halves 90 degrees.

8. Grill shrimp additional 2 to 3 minutes. Depending on the heat of your grill, the lemons may take slightly longer than the shrimp to char.

9. Plate and serve hot along with lemon halves.

TIP:
USE TWO SKEWERS FOR EACH SHRIMP KEBAB TO PREVENT SHRIMP FROM SPINNING ON A SINGLE SKEWER.

SMOKED CEDAR PLANK SALMON

I know what you're thinking. *Matt, why am I putting my perfectly good salmon on a plank of wood?* I promise, there's a reason other than Instagram photos, although I admit it makes for a great picture or two. Putting salmon on a cedar plank is a great, practical way to cook fish beautifully. The plank allows for easy handling, as salmon can split or fall into chunks when you're trying to shift or flip it on a grill. The plank is also a great way to infuse your fish with subtle smoky flavor without burning or overcooking it.

So grab a plank now (they are available online and at many retailers for next to nothing), and you'll thank me later!

1 wild salmon filet cut into 5-inch-wide pieces

1 Tbsp. olive oil

2½ tsp. BBQ rub (page 13), ½ tsp. per piece of fish

3 sprigs fresh thyme

1 lemon, sliced

1. Soak wood plank in water for one hour.
2. Light grill and set up for indirect heat at 325°F.
3. Rinse fish in cold water, and pat dry.
4. Evenly coat each piece of fish with olive oil and place fish, skin side down, on a soaked cedar plank.
5. Season each piece of fish with BBQ rub and fresh thyme, and place a slice of lemon on top.
6. Place planked fish on grill over indirect heat, close lid, and allow to cook till internal temperature reaches 135°F (about 20 minutes).
7. Remove from grill and serve on plank.

TIP:
THIS IS A VERY BASIC RECIPE THAT CAN GO IN SO MANY DIRECTIONS. I MOSTLY WANTED TO CONVEY THE SIMPLICITY OF THE TECHNIQUE AND INTRODUCE GRILLERS TO THE CONCEPT OF USING A CEDAR PLANK TO ACHIEVE A SLIGHTLY SMOKY FLAVOR IN THE SALMON. THIS TECHNIQUE IS ALSO DELICIOUS USING DIJON MUSTARD AND BROWN SUGAR AS OPPOSED TO THE BBQ RUB, OR MAPLE SYRUP AND BROWN SUGAR WITH ORANGE ZEST. THE SKY IS THE LIMIT, SO PLAY AROUND WITH VARIOUS COMBINATIONS. LET ME KNOW VIA SOCIAL MEDIA WHAT YOU COME UP WITH!

· CHAPTER EIGHT ·

SIDE DISHES

BACON-WRAPPED MAPLE-CINNAMON CARROTS

Sometimes you have to get sneaky with vegetables. Your kids may turn their nose up at a carrot, but what if it's wrapped in bacon, with a sweet hint of maple and cinnamon? You'll be amazed how fast they gobble it up.

This recipe isn't only for picky eaters; it's the perfect side dish for holiday dinners. Maple and cinnamon flavors blend with a Thanksgiving dinner or a winter meal. Plus, this sweet, crisp addition frees up much-needed room in the oven when you're scrambling to cook the rest of your feast.

The secret to perfecting this recipe is the bacon. Buy thinly sliced bacon that will crisp up quickly on the grill. Thick cuts will take too long to cook and turn the carrots to mush. And remember: a vegetable wrapped in bacon is still a vegetable, so technically you're eating healthy whenever you make this!

½ cup maple syrup

1 Tbsp. fresh ground cinnamon

2 lb. carrots (uniform in size, washed and peeled)

1 lb. thin-cut bacon

pinch of salt

1 Tbsp. finely chopped parsley, for garnish

1. Light grill and set up for indirect heat at 400°F.

2. While grill is warming up, whisk together the syrup and cinnamon.

3. Lightly coat carrots with cinnamon-syrup mixture; a basting brush works well for this task.

4. Spiral wrap each carrot with one slice of bacon. Depending on the size of the carrot, two slices may be needed.

5. Apply another coat of the cinnamon-syrup to the outside of the bacon and sprinkle with a pinch of salt.

6. Place carrots on grill over indirect heat. Ensure you lay the carrots with the tips of the bacon tucked under the carrots to prevent them from unraveling.

7. Close lid and cook for 15 minutes.

8. Open lid and reapply another coat of the cinnamon-syrup. Close lid and cook additional 15 minutes or until bacon is crisp and carrots are firm but cooked.

9. Remove from grill, drizzle with any remaining cinnamon-syrup, garnish with parsley, and serve.

BLISTERED SHISHITO PEPPERS WITH LIME AND SMOKED SALT

Every gardener has learned this the hard way: if you plant some peppers in your garden, you better be prepared to eat nothing but peppers for about three solid months. Fortunately, I've found a way to use my abundance of shishito peppers for a dish that is a delicious duel of spicy and sweet for your palate.

I drew inspiration for this recipe from an appetizer I had at a burger joint called The Cut in Orange County, California. It was love at first taste. I adapted that dish for the grill so I could infuse the peppers with a smoky flavor that gives them a depth of taste. Though they're a go-to grilling staple for me, you can make this recipe on the stovetop with a trusty cast-iron skillet. I recommend using my smoked salt on this dish, as it really adds to the smoky flavors, but sea salt will brighten up the taste just fine. The addition of honey to the finished recipe ensures that the heat of the pepper is balanced for even the most spice-sensitive eater in your family.

Once you've tried this recipe, you'll be dedicating a whole section of your garden to shishitos. You won't be sorry. This versatile little pepper is more than a great side dish; it's also an excellent topping for burgers and tacos, as well as an essential ingredient in my roasted ranch corn salsa (page 42). Dig in and embrace the pepper!

12 medium-to-large shishito peppers

1½ Tbsp. olive oil

1 tsp. honey

1 lime

2 tsp. smoked salt (page 22) or sea salt

1. Light grill and set up for high direct heat.
2. Rinse shishito peppers in cold water, and dry.
3. In small mixing bowl, combine olive oil and honey.
4. Place peppers in large mixing bowl and toss with olive oil and honey mixture, and then with juice from half a lime.
5. Place peppers directly over heat, flipping constantly until the skin begins to blister.
6. Remove from grill, plate, and squeeze juice from remaining half of lime.
7. Sprinkle with hickory or sea salt and serve hot.

CILANTRO-LIME GRILLED SWEET POTATOES

Sweet potatoes are one of my favorite vegetables, but they don't seem to find their way to the grill often. It's time for that to change.

This recipe kicks up traditional sweet potato flavor with a zesty citrus glaze. Remember to boil the sweet potato wedges before you grill them; boiling helps the flesh absorb the glaze and creates the perfect texture to finish on the grill.

Quick to cook and bursting with flavor, these are a great alternative to traditional fries that even picky eaters will fall for. It's also a healthy side dish that you can serve with confidence.

POTATOES

2 large sweet potatoes, peeled and cut into ¼-inch wedges (fry-shaped)

1 Tbsp. sea salt

GLAZE

¼ cup chopped fresh cilantro, reserving 1 tsp.

¼ cup olive oil

2 Tbsp. fresh lime juice

2 tsp. lime zest

1 tsp. soy sauce

½ tsp. savory seasoning

½ tsp. garlic powder

1. Light grill and prepare for medium direct heat.

2. Combine ingredients for glaze into mixing bowl, minus 1 teaspoon cilantro, and whisk together thoroughly.

3. In large saucepan, bring 6 cups water and 1 tablespoon salt to a hard boil. Add sweet potato wedges, return to hard boil, and cook for 3 minutes. Remove and pat dry.

4. Toss wedges with glaze until fully coated. Place on grill directly over medium heat. Grill each side until a nice dark char and grill marks form (about 5 minutes per side).

5. Remove from grill, brush on another coat of glaze, and garnish with reserved cilantro.

TIP:
CHAR SOME LIME HALVES ON THE GRILL WHILE YOU'RE GRILLING THE POTATOES AND SERVE ALONGSIDE THE POTATO WEDGES. THE CHARRED LIME JUICE BRINGS AN ADDED LAYER OF FLAVOR TO THE ALREADY DELICIOUS POTATOES.

GRILLED GARLIC BUTTER AND CHIVE HASSELBACK POTATOES

This recipe is so good, it's downright historic. Hasselback potatoes originated in eighteenth-century Sweden when a restaurant called Hasselbacken had the genius idea to slice their spuds and stuff them with flavor. By slicing the potato thinly and then cooking it, the chefs ensured that each segment was crisp and perfectly seasoned. Over the years, this crunchy, delicious recipe has changed, but we can still all thank Sweden for the idea.

My version of this classic dish is so simple and delicious, you'll be buying potatoes by the sack to make more. Be sure to evenly spread the seasoning over the sliced potato and watch the flavor unfurl as it cooks and separates on the grill. Hasselback potatoes are beautiful when served and will impress every guest at your table. Pair these spectacular spuds with any of my steak recipes for a feast that will keep your guests raving for weeks.

Want to really put this recipe over the top? Add your choice of cheese to the potato during the last 10 minutes of the bake.

4 medium russet potatoes

1 stick unsalted butter

2 cloves garlic, minced

2 Tbsp. chopped chives

2 tsp. sea salt

1. Light grill and set for indirect heat at 425°F.

2. Wash potatoes, pat dry, and make a slice about every ⅛ inch in each potato. Place potatoes between wooden spoons to act as a guide so you don't cut all the way through the potatoes.

3. Rinse potatoes in cold water to wash starch out of slices.

4. Using a fork, combine butter and minced garlic and thoroughly spread over potatoes, getting as much into the slices as possible.

5. Place on grill over indirect heat, close lid and bake for 30 minutes. Open lid and reapply butter mixture.

6. Bake for another 15–30 minutes until potatoes are crispy and they have fanned out.

7. Remove from grill, add chives and sea salt, and serve.

GRILLED ROSEMARY PARMESAN POTATOES

White potatoes have earned a bad rap in recent years. Health nuts point to the starch content and the carbs. Here's my irrefutable rebuttal: potatoes are delicious. It's true that this staple of many American dinner tables can be unhealthy if you consume them the way I did as a kid—mashed with heavy cream, butter, and cheese. But I think it's time we stop blaming the potato for delicious indulgences of the past.

This recipe is a quick, clean, and relatively healthy way to enjoy a spud side dish. Rosemary and Parmesan cheese pair beautifully to offer a slightly sophisticated take on a classic American staple.

2 to 3 large russet potatoes

¼ cup olive oil

3 Tbsp. rosemary salt (page 19)

¼ cup fresh grated Parmesan cheese

1. Set your grill up for two-zone heat at 400°F.

2. Wash potatoes and, leaving skin on, cut them into slices 1 to 1.5 inches thick.

3. Rinse in cold water to remove as much starch as possible and pat dry with paper towel.

4. Place potatoes in a large mixing bowl and add olive oil. Mix thoroughly until all slices are evenly coated.

5. Sprinkle rosemary salt on potatoes one tablespoon at a time, tossing after each tablespoon to ensure even coating.

6. Place potatoes on grill using indirect heat. Roast about 45 minutes or until they start to become lightly browned and crisp.

7. Add cheese to the top of the potatoes and continue to cook 5–7 more minutes, till cheese melts to a golden brown.

8. Remove from grill and serve warm.

TIP: THESE GO AMAZINGLY WELL WITH SEEKER SAUCE (PAGE 20).

GRILLED STREET CORN

Street corn is one of the more delicious traditional foods you can find throughout North America. From Mexico to Maryland, you can find sumptuous ears of corn adorned with local spices and cheese. This is one of those recipes that could easily go from side dish to meal, depending on how many ears you plan on eating. I can easily eat nothing but grilled street corn at summer cookouts, the recipe is that good.

Don't skip soaking the corn or grilling the limes. By soaking the ears before you cook, the corn steams while it cooks and is less likely to burn. By grilling the limes, you bring out a sweet and crisp flavor, which really brightens up the taste of the corn. Use this low-prep high-flavor dish to steal the show at any cookout you attend.

¼ cup salt, plus 1 Tbsp.

4 to 6 ears of corn, husks on

½ cup mayonnaise

2 Tbsp. extra virgin olive oil

1 tsp. pepper

2 limes, cut in half

2 cups cotija or Parmesan cheese

2 Tbsp. chopped cilantro

cayenne powder or BBQ rub (page 13)

1. In a large pot add 1 gallon of warm water and ¼ cup of salt. Submerge ears of corn in water, husks on. Soak for at least 15 minutes.

2. Light grill and set up for two-zone heat at 350°F.

3. While the grill is heating, whisk together in a bowl mayonnaise, extra virgin olive oil, remaining tablespoon of salt, and pepper.

4. Once the grill has reached 350°F, place corn on indirect side, leaving the husks on. The wet husks will steam the corn as it cooks. Grill for 25 to 30 minutes with the lid closed.

5. Remove corn from the grill. Peel husks back but do not remove them. Be careful when doing so—the steam inside the husks is hot. (Sadly I know this from experience.) Remove as much silk as possible. If using a charcoal grill, leave grill lid open to ensure coals are extremely hot for next step.

6. With husks peeled back, return corn to grill and place over direct heat. Turn corn often so as not to burn, but not so often that you don't get some nice charred kernels. This char will add to the flavor and presentation.

7. Remove from grill and allow to cool for 5 minutes before applying a thin coat of mayo mixture to corn.

8. As corn is cooling, place lime halves on the grill cut side down. Char 2–3 minutes or until they start to caramelize. Remove from grill.

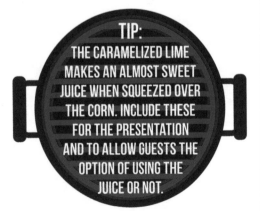

TIP:
THE CARAMELIZED LIME MAKES AN ALMOST SWEET JUICE WHEN SQUEEZED OVER THE CORN. INCLUDE THESE FOR THE PRESENTATION AND TO ALLOW GUESTS THE OPTION OF USING THE JUICE OR NOT.

9. Spoon cheese over corn to coat mayo mixture. If you are using Parmesan cheese, don't use the pre-shredded stuff; get a nice block of hard Parmesan and grate it using the fine section of a box grater.

10. To finish, top with cayenne powder, my BBQ rub, or your favorite BBQ rub. Serve with husks peeled back, and garnish with cilantro and grilled lime as desired.

PROSCIUTTO-WRAPPED GRILLED ASPARAGUS WITH BALSAMIC GLAZE

I grew up eating a ton of asparagus because we had so much of it. My dad planted it one year, and it didn't amount to much. After a couple years of cultivation and fertilizing with chicken manure (applied by yours truly—I loved that job like I love a root canal), it grew like wildfire. As a result, we ate it about every night in the summer, my mom often blanching and freezing it for the winter.

You'll find the best asparagus are the thinner spears. Once they get thicker than a number 2 pencil, they start to get tough and stringy; keep this in mind when picking them out at the grocery store or farmers market.

This recipe is super simple and makes an excellent side dish for beef, chicken, or fish, or it can serve as an appetizer on a charcuterie plate.

24 fresh asparagus spears (trim off the bottom 2 inches)

2 Tbsp. olive oil

2 Tbsp. rosemary salt (page 19)

6 thin slices prosciutto, cut lengthwise (for a total of 12 pieces)

¼ cup balsamic vinegar

1 Tbsp. sugar

pinch of cayenne powder (optional)

1. Coat trimmed asparagus with olive oil and dust with rosemary salt.

2. Wrap two spears each (total of 12 groups) with prosciutto. Wrap them around the center, leaving the bottoms and heads of the spears uncovered.

3. Light grill and prepare for high direct heat.

4. In small saucepan, bring balsamic vinegar to low boil. Whisk in sugar and small pinch of cayenne. Continue to whisk until vinegar reduces to the size of about 2 tablespoons and is the consistency of maple syrup. Set aside to cool.

5. Place wrapped spears over direct heat, grilling for 2 minutes on each side. Prosciutto should crisp up and brown slightly, and asparagus should maintain a firm crunch.

6. Remove from grill, plate, and drizzle with balsamic glaze.

SMOKED APPLE, RADISH, AND JALAPEÑO SLAW

No cookout or summer block party is complete without coleslaw. Sadly, there's always the one neighbor, or worse yet family member, who shows up with a 2-pound bucket of coleslaw from the deli counter at their local grocery store. They usually end up taking about a pound and a half of that home with them because no one wants that nasty stuff, and they likely toss it out a week or so later after it's grown a beard in their refrigerator. Don't be that person. Instead, try this incredible slaw recipe that is always a crowd favorite. It's honestly good enough to stand on its own as a solo side dish, and it's amazing as a topper to a pulled pork sandwich. For a real treat, try using it as a topping for the baked beans on page 144.

1 head green cabbage

½ gala apple, julienned

½ medium jalapeño, deseeded and thinly sliced

4 large radishes, julienned

¼ cup chopped cilantro

¼ cup mayonnaise

1 tsp. apple cider vinegar

1 tsp. smoked salt (page 22)

½ tsp. pepper

1. Light grill and set for indirect heat at 135°F.
2. Cut head of cabbage in half.
3. Add one chunk of apple wood to hot coals. If using a gas grill, use a smoke tube with pellets. Place cabbage halves over indirect heat and grill for 20 minutes. You're not trying to cook the cabbage here, just infuse it with some great smoke flavor.
4. Remove cabbage from grill and allow it to cool.
5. Using a large knife, chop cabbage into pieces roughly two inches long and ¼ inch wide.
6. Place chopped cabbage, apples, jalapeño, radish, and cilantro in a bowl. Toss to combine.
7. In a separate bowl, add mayonnaise, apple cider vinegar, salt, and pepper. Whisk until combined.
8. Pour the mayonnaise mixture over cabbage mixture and gently toss until combined.
9. Chill in refrigerator until ready to serve.

SMOKED BAKED BEANS

When I think of baked beans, I think of two things: cowboys out on the range and a neighborhood BBQ. As a young boy I had big dreams of becoming a cowboy. My mom could probably dig out pictures of me in my pajamas complete with cowboy boots, red cowboy hat, and cap gun holstered to my side. Since I do a lot of outdoor grilling and *still* like to fantasize about being a cowboy on the range (I can't believe I said that out loud), these baked beans are one of my favorite sides.

You'll love how well these beans take the smoke, giving them a rustic campfire taste. I have done this recipe with both dried beans (soaked overnight) and with precooked plain Great Northern beans from a can. I find no difference in flavor, but the canned beans are much easier to use, though slightly more expensive. Either way you make these beans, they go with burgers, hot dogs, pulled pork sandwiches, or any barbecue classic. Beans off the grill make a great sidekick.

2 Tbsp. vegetable oil

1 lb. thick-cut bacon, sliced into 1-inch pieces

4 cloves garlic, finely chopped

1 medium Vidalia onion, roughly chopped

1 medium jalapeño, seeded and roughly chopped

96 oz. canned Great Northern beans

2 cups of your favorite BBQ sauce

¼ cup molasses

¼ cup apple cider vinegar

1 cup brown sugar

2 tsp. smoked salt (page 22)

2 tsp. fresh ground pepper

1. Light grill and set up for two-zone heat at 225°F. Place a cast-iron Dutch oven directly over white-hot charcoal or gas burner.

2. Heat vegetable oil in the pan and add bacon. Cook for about 5 minutes in order to render some fat from the bacon, but avoid crisping the bacon.

3. Add the garlic, onions, and jalapeño and cook for 5 minutes, stirring constantly.

4. Add the beans, BBQ sauce, molasses, cider vinegar, brown sugar, salt, and pepper, and mix thoroughly.

5. Move Dutch oven to indirect heat as far away from hot coals or burner as possible. Place hickory chunk into the hot coals and cover grill; if using a gas grill, use a smoke tube.

6. Cook for 2 hours. Remove beans and serve.

SMOKED SWEET CORN POLENTA

As much as I love meat, I recognize that man can't live off meat alone. (OK, I probably could, but not everyone prefers a diet of meat alone.) A good side dish is key to a successful meal, and corn polenta is one of my favorites. This is traditionally done on a stovetop, but we're grilling here! Let's take this one up a notch, get it on the grill, and infuse it with a hint of mild smoke. Up until a few years ago, I had never tried polenta; truth be told, I didn't even know there was such a thing. I was at a steak house in Washington, DC, and the waiter suggested it. I skeptically went along with it, and I was hooked.

I do this from scratch, but if you want to take a shortcut, there are many precooked packages of polenta (and frozen corn) that you can purchase, which will save you some of the beginning steps of the recipe. I've tried it this way, and it's still good, just not as good. If you do opt to try it from scratch, be sure to buy coarse cornmeal that is designed for polenta, as opposed to fine cornmeal.

6-8 ears fresh unhusked sweet corn, if in season; otherwise, I use 16 oz. (about 2 cups) frozen sweet corn

3 cups vegetable stock

3 cups water

1 Tbsp. kosher salt

2 cups corn grits (polenta)

1 cup heavy cream, divided

6 Tbsp. butter

2½ cups (9 oz.) shredded Parmesan cheese, divided

2 tsp. smoked salt (page 22)

2 tsp. cayenne powder (optional)

1. Light grill and set up for indirect heat at 350°F.
2. Soak the unhusked corn in water for 30 minutes.
3. Place corn on preheated grill still in their husks. Roast for 20 minutes.
4. While the corn is roasting, in a large saucepan on the side burner, add 3 cups of vegetable stock, 3 cups of water, and 1 tablespoon of salt. Bring to a boil.
5. Take roasted corn off grill. Remove husks and cut the kernels off the corn.
6. Gradually add polenta and ½ cup heavy cream to boiling stock. Reduce heat to low and simmer for 30 minutes, stirring frequently. The polenta will have the consistency of thick mashed potatoes when finished. Note that polenta will burn if you use too much heat or if you don't stir it often.
7. Add butter, 1½ cups Parmesan cheese, and remaining ½ cup heavy cream. Stir well until the ingredients are thoroughly incorporated.
8. Add corn, smoked salt, and optional cayenne pepper. Stir until incorporated.
9. Add smoke tube of pecan pellets to your gas grill; if using a charcoal grill, use one pecan wood chunk.
10. Transfer the polenta mixture to a 14-inch cast-iron skillet or oven-safe dish. Top with remaining 1 cup Parmesan cheese and place on preheated grill. Let smoke till cheese is melted and slightly browned.
11. Garnish and serve hot.

SWEET AND SAVORY GRILLED CORN BREAD

Growing up, corn bread was a staple around my grandmother's house, along with navy beans and ham, collard greens, apple fritters, and so on. (Ya know, your typical Southern fare.) My grandmother made two versions of corn bread: one was sweet, and the other was a more traditional corn bread that my grandfather used to eat with buttermilk. I never cared for the more traditional style, but the sweet stuff always had me asking for seconds. She called the sweet cornbread "Johnny Bread," and to this day I don't know why she called it that or who Johnny was, but I do know the bread was amazing.

Over the years I have expanded on my grandmother's original recipe to include a little heat. My family was never one for the spice, so I think I picked that preference up after joining the Marines and moving to Southern California, but I digress. The point is, I have added some heat and some cheese because, as you know from the moink ball recipe on page 38, "I like cheese." After some trial and error, this is now my go-to for cornbread, and I hope it becomes yours as well.

½ cup roughly chopped bacon

1 cup flour

1 cup yellow cornmeal

¼ cup sugar

1 Tbsp. baking powder

1 tsp. kosher salt

1 cup buttermilk

1 tsp. vanilla

¼ cup butter, melted

¼ cup honey

2 eggs, room temperature and slightly beaten

1 large jalapeño pepper, seeded and minced

1½ cups shredded extra-sharp cheddar

1. Light grill and set up for indirect heat at 350°F. Grease a 12-inch cast-iron skillet and place it on the grill so that it preheats with the grill. (It's a common misconception that cast-iron heats evenly, but nothing could be further from the truth. Cast-iron holds heat extremely well, but it doesn't heat evenly whatsoever. It's important to preheat the pan for 20 minutes or so before adding the mixture, or you'll end up with random burnt portions of corn bread because of hot spots on the pan. Believe me, you're not going to want to waste a single crumb of this bread.)

2. Fry bacon till golden brown, place on paper towel to remove grease, and set aside.

3. In a large mixing bowl, combine flour, cornmeal, sugar, baking powder, and salt. Whisk together thoroughly.

4. In a separate bowl, combine buttermilk, vanilla, butter, honey, and eggs.

5. Make a well in the center of the dry ingredients and add the wet ingredients, along with bacon and jalapeño. Mix well.

6. Add cheddar and fold until evenly distributed.

7. Pour mixture into preheated cast-iron skillet.

8. Add 1 apple wood chunk to your coals; if using a gas grill, use a smoke tube with apple pellets. Place cast-iron pan over indirect heat for about 20 minutes or until you can slide a toothpick in and pull it out clean.

9. Glaze the top of the cornbread with a light coat of melted butter and let cook an additional 3–5 minutes. This adds a little flavor and a beautiful top crust.

10. Let cool 15 minutes before slicing and serving directly from the cast-iron pan.

• CHAPTER NINE •

DESSERTS

GRILLED ANGEL FOOD CAKE WITH STRAWBERRY PUREE

I have a confession to make. As a young man, I was a strawberry thief. I couldn't get enough of the sweet summer fruit and was known to pilfer from local gardens. Luckily, I had understanding neighbors, like Mr. Simmons, who taught me how to grow strawberries for myself.

I'm reformed now, which is why I like this guilt-free summer dessert that's more on the angelic side. Grilling angel food cake brings an irresistible texture and flavor to an often-bland dessert. Though I use my beloved strawberries for the puree, you can substitute any seasonal berry that you prefer. Fresh fruit is always better, but if your favorite berries are out of season, you can pick up a pack of frozen berries and still get great results. If you're looking for a way to cut a few calories from the recipe, use a sugar substitute.

Remember to save your leftover puree for biscuits, or shortbreads, or just to eat out of the container with a spoon. It's that good.

1 store-bought angel food cake

2 pints fresh strawberries (about 5 cups)

½ cup sugar

2 cups whipped cream

mint (to garnish)

1. Light grill and set up for medium-high direct heat.

2. Wash strawberries and remove stems. Set aside half of one pint.

3. Place remaining strawberries and sugar in a food processor or bullet-style blender and blend 30 seconds or until the strawberries become a puree. Pour into sealable container and leave at room temperature. Any leftover puree can be stored in the refrigerator for a few days.

4. Slice angel food cake into 3-inch thick pieces.

5. Place pieces of angel food cake over direct heat, grilling about 2 minutes per side, or until cake becomes lightly charred and toasted.

6. Plate along with fresh whole strawberries and whipped cream. Drizzle with strawberry puree, and garnish with mint.

GRILLED PEACH BOATS WITH MASCARPONE ICE CREAM

This is the holy grail of summer desserts. It's sweet, it's pretty to look at, kids love it, and it's healthy. (That last part surprised me too.)

Grilling a fresh peach brings out a deeper flavor in the sweet summer fruit. Juicy peaches pair perfectly with the subtle flavors of the mascarpone mixture. If you're in a rush, this recipe works just fine with any mild-flavored ice cream. You're serving up bright flavors and natural sweetness, so you won't mind when your kids beg you for seconds.

3 peaches, cut in half

1 cup mascarpone cheese

¼ cup powdered sugar

2 tsp. ground cinnamon

1 tsp. vanilla extract

1½ cups heavy whipping cream

2 Tbsp. graham cracker crumbs

2 Tbsp. maple syrup

1. Light grill and prepare for direct heat.
2. Add mascarpone cheese, powdered sugar, cinnamon, and vanilla extract to a large bowl and beat with a hand mixer.
3. Add in heavy whipping cream and beat until fluffy. Place in refrigerator.
4. Place each peach half on grill over direct heat, cut side down. Grill till charred (about 2 minutes). Turn and grill other side for additional 90 seconds.
5. Remove from grill, fill each peach with mascarpone, and top with a dusting of graham crackers and a drizzle of maple syrup.

GRILLED PEANUT BUTTER BANANA SPLIT

Elvis wasn't the only guy who loved a grilled peanut butter and banana sandwich—I grew up on that ooey gooey treat myself. My fond memories of that sandwich inspired this unconventional banana split, which is a hit with adults and kids alike. I decided to up the ante on the indulgence, grilling the bananas to bring out extra sweetness. Substituting marshmallows for ice cream gives you more time to savor the flavors.

The best part of this dish? There's no cleanup. Split the banana in half and use the peel as a serving dish. It's an impressive presentation and one less dish to wash.

4 ripe bananas

1 cup peanut butter baking chips

1 cup mini marshmallows

¼ cup brown sugar

1. Light grill and set up for indirect heat at 325°F.
2. Leaving banana in peel, slice down the length of the banana, but don't cut it in half.
3. Pry apart the bananas and evenly distribute brown sugar inside each banana.
4. On top of the brown sugar, evenly distribute the peanut butter chips.
5. On top of peanut butter chips, place the mini marshmallows.
6. Place bananas in grill, close lid, and cook for 10 minutes or until peanut better chips have melted and marshmallows are toasted.
7. Remove and serve hot.

GRILLED PEARS WITH GORGONZOLA, HONEY, AND WALNUTS

Of all the grilled deserts I've made over the years, this one might be my favorite. Maybe because it reminds me of late summers spent eating pears in my grandparents' backyard picked right off their trees. Or maybe it's the memories of eating warm sweet pears over the winter that my grandmother canned after the late-summer harvest and stored in her basement. Whatever the reason, I love pears. If you've read my recipe for moink balls on page 38, you'll also know that I like cheese, so putting these two together is a no-brainer. As a kid, I had something similar to this (oven-baked) with ingredients that were all local: honey from my uncle's bee hives, walnuts that we collected from various trees—but the gorgonzola cheese is something I started adding in the last ten years or so. Admittedly, gorgonzola isn't everyone's favorite, so for those who don't like "stinky cheese" as my daughter calls it, you can substitute brie, and it's still spectacular.

3 pears, ripe but firm

2 cups baby arugula

½ cup crumbled gorgonzola cheese

¼ cup honey

¼ cup craisins

¼ cup candied walnuts

1 Tbsp. olive oil

1½ tsp. ground cinnamon

1. Light grill and set up for two-zone cooking at 425°F.

2. Cut each pear in half, remove the core, and dig small "bowl" in each pear half with a standard kitchen spoon or melon baller.

3. Coat each pear half with a light drizzle of olive oil.

4. Place pears cut side down over direct heat and grill for 2–3 minutes or until a light char and grill marks start to form. Turn pears over and move to indirect heat.

5. Fill each pear bowl with a heaping portion of gorgonzola cheese.

6. Close lid and allow pears to cook until cheese starts to melt, about 5 minutes.

7. Remove from grill and plate each pear half on a bed of baby arugula.

8. Drizzle with honey, dust with cinnamon, and garnish with craisins and candied walnuts.

GRILLED PINEAPPLE RINGS WITH ICE CREAM

One of my favorite summer recipes, this dessert is bright, fresh, and full of flavor. Grilling the pineapple produces a sweet tropical flavor that complements ice cream perfectly. Plus, pineapple is a fruit, so I'm pretty sure this counts as health food.

A breeze to make on the grill and the great way to cap off the perfect summer cookout, this ice cream sundae is customizable. Challenge your family to think of new flavor combinations for the pineapple, or just use this tested and approved recipe. I recommend using fresh pineapple, but if you want to save time (or grill up a little taste of summer during the winter months), canned pineapple rings can work too.

1 whole pineapple, sliced into 6 equal slices

6 scoops vanilla bean ice cream

6 spoonfuls of whipped cream

¼ cup almond slivers, toasted

¼ cup sweetened shredded coconut, toasted

½ cup caramel sauce

mint (to garnish)

1. Light grill and prepare for direct heat.
2. Grill pineapple until a nice char forms, about 2 minutes per side.
3. Remove pineapple from grill, top each slice with a scoop of ice cream, a dollop of whipped cream, almonds, and coconut.
4. Drizzle each with caramel sauce, garnish with mint, and serve.

TIP:
IF YOU HAVEN'T PROCESSED A WHOLE PINEAPPLE BEFORE, IT'S SUPER EASY. POSITION THE FRUIT ON ITS SIDE, AND START WITH CUTTING OFF THE TOP STEM AND THE BOTTOM. THEN STAND THE PINEAPPLE ON ITS BOTTOM AND REMOVE THE SKIN BY BY VERTICALLY SLICING IT AS THIN AS POSSIBLE. THE SWEETEST PART OF THE FRUIT IS THAT CLOSEST TO THE SKIN, SO YOU'LL WANT TO KEEP AS MUCH OF THAT FLESH AS POSSIBLE.

S'MORTILLAS

S'mores are classic treats that were made for the grill. But there are a few drawbacks to the original recipe we learned around the campfire: the graham crackers, while a great flavor, are a terrible base for this gooey dessert. They crumble, they crack, and the filling goes everywhere. In the end, you're a sticky mess coated in graham cracker crumbs.

I offer you the adult solution to your s'mores craving: tortillas. By using a tortilla instead of a graham cracker, you eliminate the mess, keep the gooey filling where it belongs, and get a great new flavor profile that brings a little sophistication to a simple treat.

I like using dark chocolate to balance the sweetness of the marshmallows, but if you're in the mood for a real childhood flashback, find your favorite milk chocolate bar.

4 large flour tortillas

1 cup dark chocolate chips

1 cup crushed graham crackers

2 cups mini marshmallows

1. Light grill and set up for indirect heat at 325°F.
2. Spread chocolate chips evenly over half of each tortilla.
3. Sprinkle crushed graham crackers evenly over chocolate.
4. Place marshmallows on chocolate. Fold the other half of the tortilla over, on top of the marshmallows.
5. Place on grill, close lid, and cook for 7 minutes or until marshmallows melt.
6. Remove, cut each tortilla into three triangle shapes, and serve warm.

SMOKED APPLE CRUMBLE

Here's a recipe that transports me to my childhood. My mother used to pick Granny Smith apples from my grandmother's trees and bake this dessert throughout the fall. Sharp and sweet, the smell of sugar and apples makes me feel like a kid again with every sniff. I haven't changed much about mom's recipe: I substituted Honeycrisp apples for Granny Smith because the flavor is a little more complex, and—of course—I moved the whole dish from the oven to the grill.

You're thinking, "This dish has been baked in ovens for years, Matt. Why am I grilling it?" Well, there are two reasons. First, I live by the philosophy "If you can cook it, you can grill it." That means I've put just about every imaginable recipe on my grill to see if it works. You'd be surprised how many do. (We'll not talk about that disastrous attempt at ice cream making.)

Second, by adding pecan wood to the grill, you augment the apple flavors of the crumble with a smoky flavor that makes this dish something unique. Sorry, Mom, but I think I might have improved upon your recipe.

Try serving this dish after my pork chop recipe (page 12). If you configure the grill for smoking after you take the chops off, this dessert can cook while you're eating.

FILLING

4-5 large Honeycrisp apples, peeled and sliced

juice from ½ lemon

2 Tbsp. flour

⅓ cup sugar

1 Tbsp. ground cinnamon

1 tsp. ground nutmeg

TOPPING

1 cup brown sugar

½ cup flour

½ cup oatmeal

½ cup caramel baking chips

¼ cup candied pecans

1 Tbsp. ground cinnamon

1 tsp. baking powder

½ tsp. salt

½ cup salted butter, cold and cut into small chunks

1. Light grill and set up for indirect heat at 350°F.

2. Place apples in a large mixing bowl and toss with lemon juice. Then add in flour, sugar, cinnamon, and nutmeg, and mix thoroughly.

3. Pour apples into a greased cast-iron pan. Set mixture aside.

4. Using the now-empty mixing bowl, combine brown sugar, flour, oatmeal, caramel chips, pecans, cinnamon, baking powder, and salt for the topping.

5. Using a pastry blender or large fork, cut the cold butter into the topping mix.

6. Cover apples with topping mixture.

7. Add one or two pecan wood chunks to the hot coals; if using a gas grill, use a smoke tube with pecan pellets. Place apple crumble over indirect heat.

8. Close lid and bake until apples start to bubble and topping begins to brown (about 45 minutes).

9. Remove from grill and serve warm with French vanilla ice cream.

SMOKED MINT CHOCOLATE MINI LAVA CAKES

I love mint chocolate ice cream. If you do too, this is the perfect dessert for you. If you're not a fan of the mint, simply leave out the mint extract. This is a great dish for summer when you have fresh fruit, and using the grill incorporates a mild smoke flavor without overpowering the chocolate. Using the outdoor grill also keeps your house cool in the summer because you're not heating up the oven. Be sure to use a mild wood like pecan or the smoke flavor will be too intense. Because we are baking on the grill, temperature control will be important, so be sure you know your grill and how it behaves in order to maintain a consistent temperature throughout the baking process.

1 stick unsalted butter

¾ cup semisweet chocolate chips

1½ cup powdered sugar

3 large whole eggs

3 egg yolks

1 tsp. vanilla extract

1 tsp. mint extract

½ tsp. kosher salt

½ cup flour

2 Tbsp. cocoa powder

fresh strawberries to garnish

1. Light grill and set for indirect heat at 375°F.
2. Spray four ramekins with nonstick cooking spray and place on a baking sheet.
3. In a large microwave-safe bowl, add butter and chocolate chips. Heat in microwave until completely melted, stirring every 30 seconds.
4. Add powdered sugar (reserving 1 tablespoon) to melted butter and chocolate and stir until fully incorporated.
5. To the chocolate mixture, gradually add 3 whole eggs, 3 egg yolks, vanilla, mint extract, and salt and stir until incorporated.
6. Add in the flour and cocoa powder and mix well.
7. Pour the mixture equally into the four ramekins.
8. Add pecan wood chunk to hot coals, and place ramekins on grill over indirect heat. Close lid and bake for 13–15 minutes. Remove from heat and let stand 1 minute.
9. Invert ramekins onto individual plates while cakes are still warm. You may have to use a butter knife and circle the outside diameter of the cake to get it to release from the bowl.
10. Sift powdered sugar over the top and serve with fresh strawberries.

INDEX

ABOUT THE AUTHOR

MATT EADS is on a mission to prove that grilling can and should be an everyday pleasure. His modest upbringing taught him you don't need fancy equipment or expensive ingredients, and his father's barbecue misadventures showed him you don't always get it right the first time. During his 13 years in the Marines, Matt continued to hone his skills, grilling for fellow Marines using his imagination and whatever was on sale at the commissary. Through subsequent careers as a stay-at-home dad and college student, corporate executive, and entrepreneur, Matt had to become more efficient to get time in front of the grill. He developed techniques and recipes that allowed him to grill every day, not just on special occasions. When Matt began sharing on Instagram, he quickly inspired tens of thousands of followers to get cooking. He created Grillseeker.com, a site filled with recipes, reviews, and tips for grillers at every skill level. Matt's years of practical application, experiments, and study help him lead fellow grillers in a stress-free celebration of good food every day, using any grill available.

 www.grillseeker.com